CREATING CERAMIC MINIATURES

CREATING CERAMIC MINIATURES

Techniques and Inspiration for Making Miniature Tableware, Figures, Ornaments, Scenes, Animals, Birds, and All Sorts of Pottery Pots, Vases, and Bowls

by CARLA and JOHN B. KENNY

CROWN PUBLISHERS, INC.   NEW YORK

All photographs by the authors unless otherwise noted.

Inquiries should be addressed to Crown Publishers, Inc., One Park Avenue,
New York, N.Y. 10016

Printed in the United States of America
Published simultaneously in Canada by
General Publishing Company Limited

Library of Congress Cataloging in Publication Data

Kenny, Carla.
Creating ceramic miniatures.

Includes index.

1. Pottery craft.   2. Miniature objects.
I. Kenny, John B., joint author.   II. Title.
TT920.K45   738   79-17027
ISBN 0-517-53591-2
ISBN 0-517-53592-0 pbk.

CONTENTS

Acknowledgments

- to all of the artists and craftsmen who welcomed us into their studios, allowed us to photograph them at their work, and took time out to discuss philosophy with us;

- to the artists who sent us photographs of their work;

- to the Metropolitan Museum of Art, New York City, whose staff was most helpful;

- to the manufacturers who supplied us with information about kilns and studio equipment;

- to Ed Walsh of AMACO who was most generous in supplying us with materials especially suited to the work of ceramic miniaturists; and,

- to Brandt Aymar, our editor, for his encouragement and his patience, our sincerest thanks.

C.K. and J.B.K.

FOREWORD

IN THIS BOOK we deal with a very special branch of ceramic art. This is a how-to book, of course, but it is also, in a way, a book about philosophy—the finding of large rewards in small things.

In the pages that follow we shall get to know a number of ceramic artists who create miniatures, some of them just for the fun of it or as a change of pace now and then to break the rhythm of making great big pots. Others are professional miniaturists who earn their living by making and selling figurines, miniature houses and landscapes, tiny figures of animals and people, as well as miniature made-to-scale furnishings for dollhouses (the scale used is $1'' = 1'$).

These artists enjoy the challenge of creating tiny environments; they share an appreciation of the charm and fascination of a miniscule world of the imagination where one may relax in a garden no bigger than a saucer or sit on a bench in a park in the shade of a miniature tree beside a tiny pool with a sparkling fountain.

We are going to visit these artists in their studios to watch them as they work. We'll interrupt them now and then to ask what materials they're using and why. And then we'll take a coffee break and talk about the fantasies and the emotions involved in creating miniature ceramics.

PLATE 1. Primitive female figures. Terra-cotta, Cypriote,
2000–1200 B.C. The Metropolitan Museum of Art, The
Cesnola Collection, purchased by subscription, 1874–76.

INTRODUCTION

HOW LONG AGO was it that mankind discovered the magic that happens when clay and fire meet? We don't know for sure, but we can be certain that it was many thousands of years. Take a look at the two stylishly coiffed terra-cotta damsels shown in plate 1. These two women are fertility goddesses made in Cypress sometime between 2000 and 1200 B.C. The one on the left is 5″ tall, her companion is an inch taller. If a farmer had one of these figurines in his home and treated her respectfully, she would see to it that his crops flourished and his herds (and his family) increased. How's that for magic?

Now for another kind of magic. In Egypt, in China, and in parts of the Middle East, powerful potentates fearing loneliness after death would take with them to the other world large retinues of servitors, musicians, entertainers, wives, horses, and so on. There was, however, probably more involved here than a desire for company. Powerful potentates lived in constant danger of assassination by their closest associates. We can imagine a tender love scene between P.P. and one of his wives. "Dearest one," he murmurs to her, "I love you so much; I cannot bear to part from you, so I have given orders that you shall share my tomb when I die." This might give Dearest One second thoughts about that vial of poison smuggled to her by one of her favorite courtiers. Eventually, opposition to live interment forced them to substitute effigies made of various materials—wood, metal, and, of course, ceramics. These were miniature replicas of the real thing.

This produced a less grim kind of magic. Let's consider a not-so-powerful person (we'll call him Ah-met), a man of the working class who could not afford even one servant. He could still have a faithful servitor to make his life easier in the other world—a shawabti (or ushabti). This figurine, about 5″ or 6″ tall, holds a tool in one hand and a rope in the other. He is made of clay glazed with a beautiful turquoise blue. On his back is a message written in black pigment, instructing him to speak up and say "Here am I, master" whenever Ah-met is called upon to do any menial tasks.

In plate 2 is a fun figure, a terra-cotta actor, 3½″ tall, that was buried in an Athenian grave, probably around 500 B.C. Despite his glum expression, he looks like a comedian. His owner was probably a theatre buff who wanted to make sure that in the other world he would have a congenial companion.

But enough of death. Let's skip to the world of elegance that was Europe in the sixteenth, seventeenth, and eighteenth centuries when the art of making porcelain figurines reached a high point, when the artist-craftsmen of Meissen, Staffordshire, Chelsea, and other pottery centers and their imitators in China produced the exquisite figurines so treasured by collectors today. Plates 3 and 4 show two Chelsea porcelains: the cat is

PLATE 2. Statuette of actor. From Athenian grave. Height 3½". Terra-cotta, Greek, probably fourth century B.C. The Metropolitan Museum of Art, Rogers Fund, 1913.

PLATE 3. Cat. Height 3". Porcelain, English (Chelsea), c. 1775. The Metropolitan Museum of Art, Gift of Irwin Untermeyer, 1964.

INTRODUCTION

3″ tall, the children building a house of cards is 2⅞″ high. These are perfume bottles.

Plates 5 through 15 are from the collection of Mr. and Mrs. Thomas Naegele.

Porcelain figurines are in style again, as evidenced by the advertisements appearing in our sophisticated magazines. These figurines are executed with realistic precision and an abundance of accurate detail; some of them are beautifully designed. Perhaps a few years from now these too will become collectors' items.

PLATE 4. Children building house of cards. Height 2⅞″. Porcelain, English (Chelsea), c. 1760. The Metropolitan Museum of Art, Gift of Irwin Untermeyer, 1964.

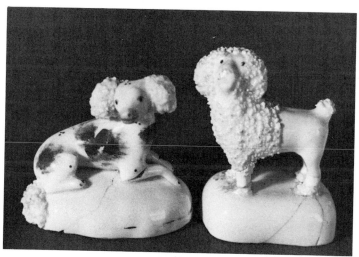

PLATE 5. Dogs. Height 2¼″. Porcelain, English, eighteenth century.

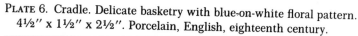

PLATE 6. Cradle. Delicate basketry with blue-on-white floral pattern. 4½″ x 1½″ x 2½″. Porcelain, English, eighteenth century.

PLATE 7. Baronial house ornamented with flowers. White porcelain with gold-luster tracings. 4½" x 3" x 5½". Eighteenth-century "air freshener."

PLATE 8. Rear view of the air freshener showing where incense was burned so its fragrance could drift out through the openings in the cupolas.

PLATE 9. Another air freshener with colorful floral trim and gold-luster accents. Height 3". Porcelain, English, eighteenth century.

PLATE 10. Castle. 5½" x 4¾" x 7". Air freshener with delicate floral trim with gold-luster tracings on turrets and windows. Porcelain, English, eighteenth century.

PLATE 11. Cherubs with baskets of flowers. Height 4½". Porcelain, English (Chelsea), eighteenth century.

PLATE 12. Little rich boy (left). Height 4½". Runaway boy. Height 3½". Meissen ware, eighteenth century.

PLATE 13. Man on goat. Height 4½". Porcelain, English (Chelsea), eighteenth century.

PLATE 14. Porcelain cup. English, eighteenth century. Mark "Coalport, 1750." A rare item.

PLATE 15. Porcelain head. Height 3″. English (Chelsea), eighteenth century.

chapter · 1

CLAY: TEST AND PINCH

TOOLS FOR THE MINIATURE CERAMIST

ARTISTS have a tendency to collect too many tools, and the frustration of "which one is best" is apt to deter productive creativity. So, we recommend that the miniaturist be selective, start with just a few tools—begin first by finding out what can be done with the fingers!

A most useful tool would be one to help in the forming of clay, the potter's smallest wooden tool that has one flat end and a ball end.

Things found in the home are often useful—a small crochet hook, a paring knife, emery boards for final cleaning of the edges of a bone-dry piece.

A sponge (preferably a little silk sponge from a ceramic supply shop), a spray bottle of water, a small workboard and a 14″ square of oilcloth with cotton backing to work on are good to have.

After the artist becomes more familiar with clay and his imagination begins to take flight, he may want to expand his collection of implements and equipment—old dental tools with crooked sharp ends for cutting and cleaning hard-to-get-at corners; a small fine metal file that is rounded at both ends; and for ornamental pressings such objects as tiny carved buttons and beads, seedpods, pinecones, acorns, and other things that would give interesting textures when pressed against wet clay.

Keeping tools moist and clean while working is most important since clay tends to cling to what it touches.

CLAY BODIES

To make miniatures we need clay that is plastic enough to be easily shaped and still tough enough to stand on its own. We could get our clay by digging it from the ground, but it is much easier for us if we start by buying some.

The catalogs of ceramic supply dealers offer a large variety of clays and clay bodies (the term *clay* means a substance just as it is dug from the ground, while *clay body* is clay to which things have been added to improve its working quality or its color or its firing range). Clay can be bought in powdered or moist form. We shall start with a prepared white talc, low-firing clay body bought from a dealer:

PHOTO SERIES 1: *Testing a Clay Body*

1. Our miniature studio. The working surface is a piece of plywood 14″ square. To the right is a plaster bat that fits on top of a small kitchen turntable. A dish holds a moistened sponge. Tools are a modeling tool, a potter's knife, and a small crochet hook. We have a bag of clay and some paper towels.

2. A lump of clay about the size of a golf ball is cut in half.

3. The two halves have been laid one on top of the other and pressed together. This is the process of *wedging*, about the best method there is of mixing clay.

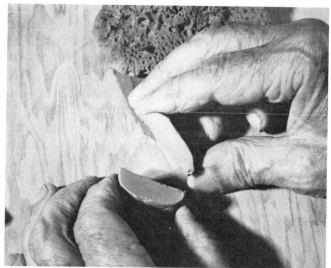

4. The clay came to us thoroughly wedged, but after we have worked with it for a while and returned it to its bag, it will need more wedging before we work with it again. If we cut a lump in half and then squeeze the two halves together, one on top of the other, and continue doing this a few times, the clay should be thoroughly mixed. To check, we cut the lump in half and look at the surface of the cut. If it contains no irregular striations and no air pockets, it is in good condition for working.

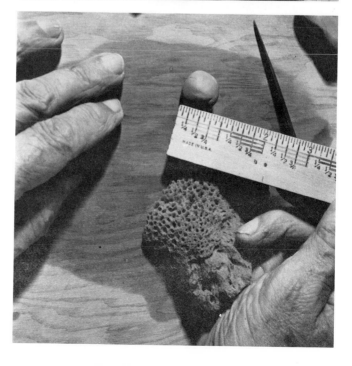

5. A ball of clay has been rolled until it is ½″ in diameter.

6. The ball of clay is then rolled into a rope shape. The board on which rolling is done is kept damp with the sponge. As the fingers roll they separate. If our clay has good working properties, we should be able to roll the ½″ ball into a thin rope of clay 3″ long.

7. Another lump of clay is being rolled into a long thin rope.

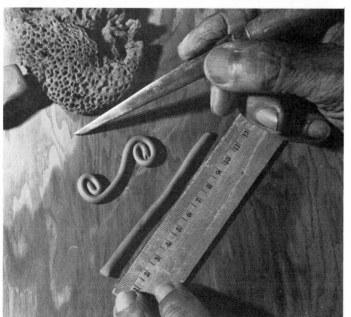

8. The long thin rope has been twisted into a scroll shape shown in the center. This means that the clay has excellent plasticity. The 3″ strip of clay has been cut to a length of 10 centimeters. This strip will tell the percentage of shrinkage of the clay after drying and after firing.

PHOTO SERIES 2: *Making a Miniature Pinch Pot*

Usually pinch pots are made by taking a ball of clay about the size of a golf ball in the palm of one hand, pressing the index finger of the other hand into the center, working to make the sides of the little bowl taller and thinner. This is an excellent exercise for getting to know your clay. The results are often beautiful (note the pinch pots by Alan Schnepel in the color section):

1. A tiny ball of clay has been rolled.

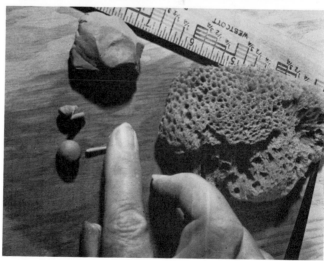

2. A strip for the foot is rolled.

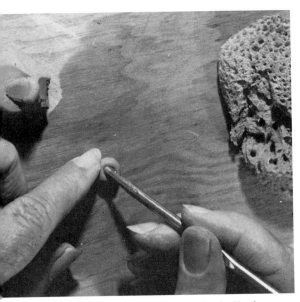

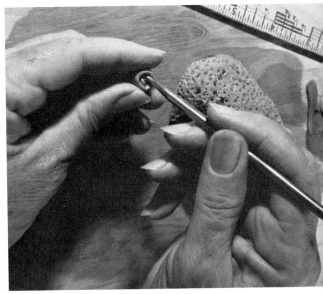

3. An opening is made in the ball of clay using the crochet hook.

4. The opening is enlarged and the wall of the bowl is made thinner.

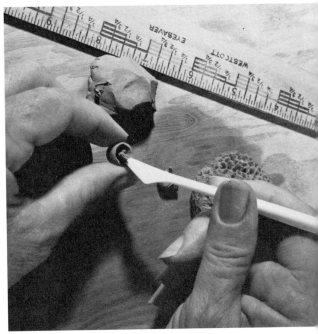

5. A tiny strip of clay is fastened on the underside to serve as a base (foot).

6. Removing excess clay from the inside.

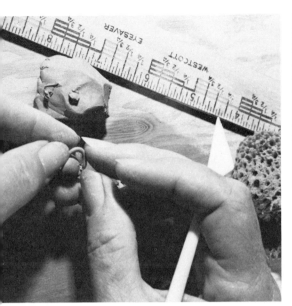 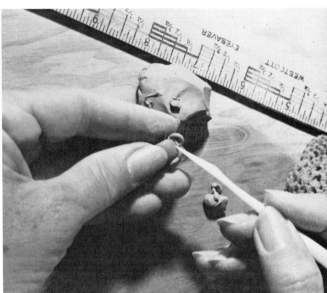

7. Attaching a handle.

8. Completing attachment of the handle.

9. The finished cup, fired and glazed, is ¼″ tall. Its saucer is 7/16″ in diameter. The dinner plate shown is ⅞″ in diameter.

SCALE

Ceramists who make miniatures for dollhouses must work to the scale of $1'' = 1'$, in other words, one-twelfth of life size. It would take some complicated arithmetic to figure what the equivalent of a 7/16″ saucer in miniature would be life size, but a ruler with inches divided into twelfths solves the problem. Plate 1-1 shows such a ruler measuring a casserole. The casserole has a diameter of 14/12″; it therefore corresponds to a 14″ casserole life size. A ruler of this type may be purchased in an art supply store, but if you prefer, you can make your own by tracing (or cutting out) the diagram in the Appendix.

PHOTO SERIES 3:   *A Mini-Pitcher*

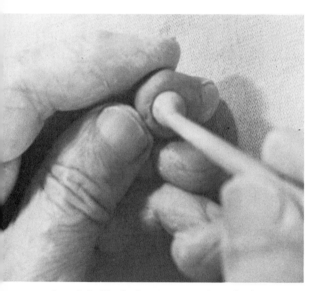

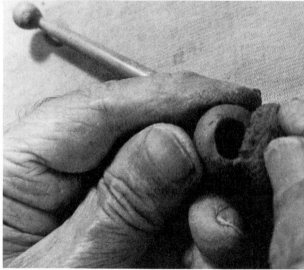

1. A ball of clay is opened with the end of a modeling tool.

2. The bowl shape is smoothed and moistened.

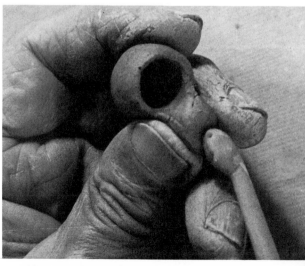

3. Adding a spout.

4. Shaping the spout.

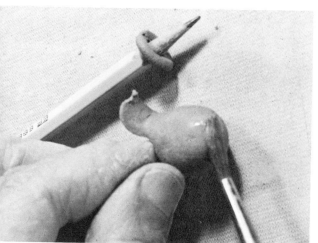

5. A tiny rope of clay has been rolled and coiled around the tip of a pencil. This will serve as a base. Bottom of the pitcher is moistened with a brush.

6. Attaching the base.

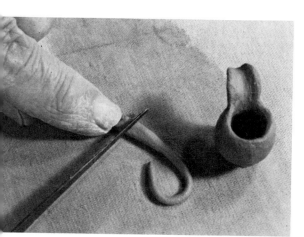

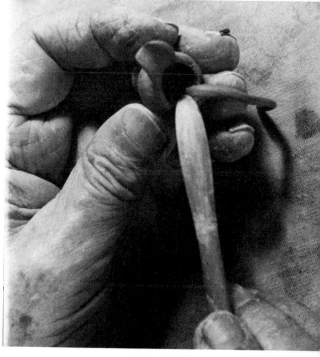

7. A strip of clay has been rolled to form a handle. It is cut to proper size.

8. Attaching the top portion of the handle to the inner side of the rim.

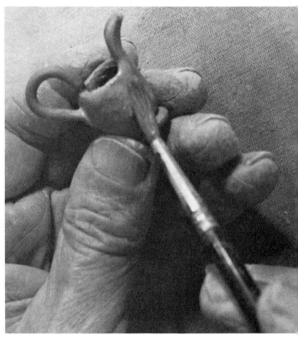

9. Attaching the lower end of the handle.

10. Smoothing the surface with a wet brush.

11. The finished pitcher, fired, glazed, and decorated with an over-glaze design. Height 1⅜".

SHRINKAGE

Clay shrinks as it dries, and it shrinks again when it is fired. Most clays shrink about 8 percent when they dry and another 8 percent when they are fired.

All of our work up to this point has been done with a commercially prepared white talc low-fire clay body that shrinks 5 percent as it dries. The shrinkage after firing is so small as to be almost imperceptible. This has enabled us to do things that would be impossible with other clays. When we come to the section on molds, we shall see that pressings or castings can be altered considerably when they are in the leather-hard or even in the bone-dry state. This has made our work much easier. See figure 1-1.

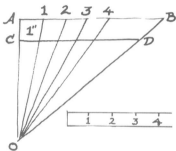

FIGURE 1-1

MAKING A SHRINKAGE RULE

Make a tile of plastic clay. On it draw a line and measure it. Fire the tile and measure the line again. Make a drawing as shown in the diagram.

- Draw line *AB* equal to the original length.
- Draw line *CD* parallel to *AB* and equal to the fired length.
- Draw lines *AC* and *BD;* prolong them until they meet at point *O.*
- On *CD* measure 1″ distances.
- Draw lines from *O* through the points laid off on *CD* and extend them until they touch line *AB.* The distance between each pair of points on *AB* shows how long a piece of clay would have to be when wet in order to be 1″ long after firing.

Mark these distances on a piece of heavy cardboard and number them *1, 2, 3 . . .* This is a shrinkage rule which can be used to measure plastic clay. The reading will show what size the clay will be when fired.

Charlie Brown is noted for his mini-pinch-pots. Let's watch him at work:

PHOTO SERIES 4: *A Spherical Form Made by Joining Two Pinch Pots*

1. The artist starts with two balls of clay, each ½″ in diameter. Each ball is pinched into a bowl shape.

2. The two bowls are pressed together. Care must be taken when the two clay forms are joined: edges that are to be pressed together should be roughened slightly and moistened with water or *slip* (clay in liquid form) or what potters call *slurry*, clay wet enough to make a kind of thick paste.

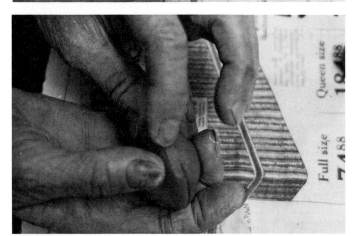

3. The artist smoothes the joint with his finger.

4. More smoothing of the joint is done with a flexible scraper.

5.   A pencil point is used to make an opening in the top.

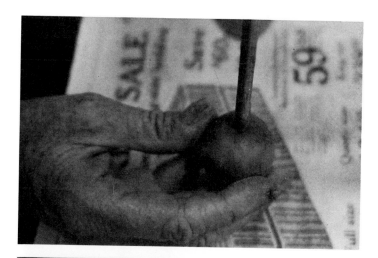

6.   A series of smaller perforations is made with the pointed end of an orangewood stick. When the piece is leather hard (not completely dry, but firm enough so that it can be handled easily and polished with a tool), the artist will *burnish* it by rubbing the surface with a bone burnishing tool, or a smooth stone. Burnishing is an ancient method of decorating pottery. After it has been fired, a burnished piece looks as if it had been glazed. Designs on ware can be made by burnishing a leather-hard surface, then scraping away portions to provide an interesting contrast between different areas of the surface of the pot.

After the pot was thoroughly dry, Charlie fired it by the raku method (see chapter 12).

The finished pot, 1½″ in diameter, is shown on the left in plate 1-2.

Miniature pinch pots, 1″ tall or smaller, may have an infinite variety of shapes. They need not all be circular, by any means. Clay can be pinched into cubes, cylinders, almost any shape; it can be pulled and twisted. On the surfaces of mini-pinch-pots we can experiment with textures, incisions, pressing in and adding on. There is no limit to what can be done (plate 1-3).

Working this way develops one's knowledge of clay, creates a rapport between clay and potter. We can learn a lot from exercises such as this and derive a great deal of pleasure from them at the same time.

PLATE 1-1

PLATE 1-2

PLATE 1-3

chapter · 2

METHODS OF FORMING

COIL BUILDING

IN THIS METHOD ropes of clay are rolled, then placed one on top of another to build up a pottery form. The method can be used to make pieces of almost any size. Care must be taken to see to it that when one coil is laid on top of another, the joint is made firm enough so that the coils will not separate during the drying and firing.

PHOTO SERIES 5: *A Coil-Built Miniature Mirror Frame*

Irene Batt makes many of her creations by the coil-building method. She keeps a jar of slurry with an old brush placed in it to serve almost as a ceramic "glue" pot.

1. In this picture she has rolled a short rope of clay and formed it into a circle. Where the rope ends join, she has used slurry as an adhesive. Now she is brushing slurry on top of the ring.

2.   A second coil is put into place.

3.   A tiny coil is looped on. This is the beginning of the creation of an original design.

4.   More tiny coils complete the design on what will be the top portion of the frame.

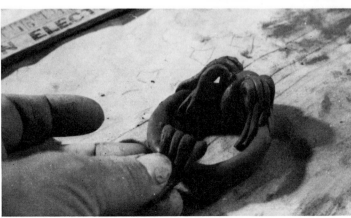

5.   The design is completed by the addition of more tiny coils to the bottom of the frame.

6. This mini-mirror-frame was fired
by the raku method.

Irene Batt sometimes uses the coil method without rolling ropes of clay, preferring to make her coils out of strips cut from a layer that has been rolled out with a rolling pin. Let's watch as she makes a miniature candle holder:

PHOTO SERIES 6: *Miniature Candelabrum*

1. A layer of clay has been rolled. A strip cut from the layer has been bent to form part of a circle (lower right). Here the artist cuts tiny discs of clay from the rolled layer. She uses a special punch cutter (a die-punch tool) made for ceramists).

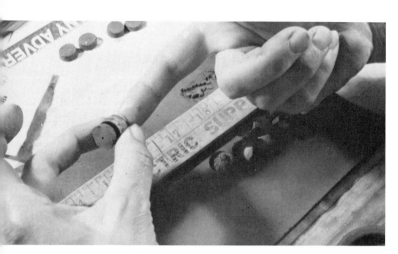

2. The punch cutter has a part that can be pressed from the top to eject the disc of clay.

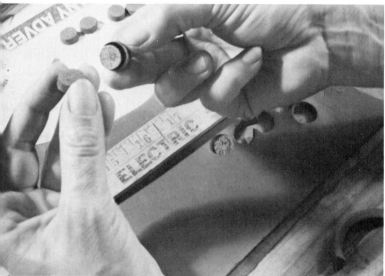

3. This picture shows the punch cutter and the ejected disc. (The edge of the cutter must be moistened beforehand each time it is used.)

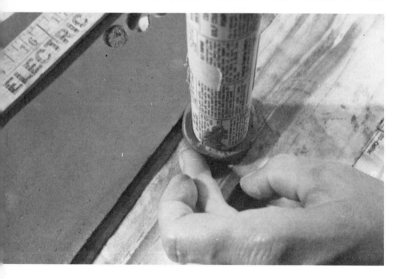

4. Several layers of newspaper have been wrapped around a narrow cardboard mailing tube. This tube will serve as a cylinder around which coils can be shaped.

5. The artist used a leather-punching tool to make holes in the center of the cut-out discs. The first coil wrapped around the mailing tube is seen in the upper left corner.

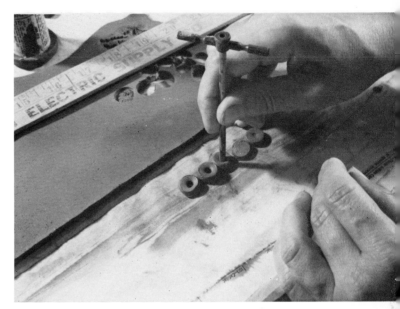

6. Slurry is brushed on the coil and perforated discs are placed on top of the coil.

7. A second row of discs is put on top of the first. The punch tool helps to position the discs.

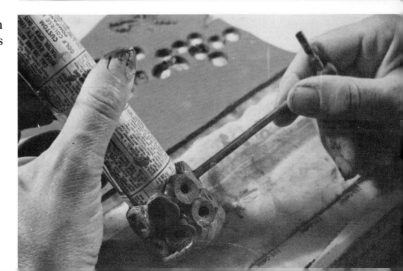

8. A second strip is coiled around the mailing tube.

9. The purpose of the newspaper wrapped around the tube is to simplify the removal of the tube from the clay form. Here the artist slides the cardboard tube out of its newspaper sleeve.

10. After the cardboard core has been taken out, removing the newspaper sleeve is no problem.

11. The artist presses the work gently so that instead of remaining circular it becomes elliptical.

12. More discs are cut and perforated. These will make the actual candle holders.

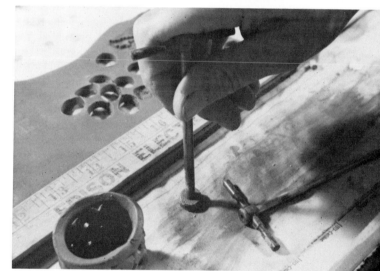

13. Tiny triangular shapes are cut from the clay layer.

14. A triangle is fastened to a perforated disc.

15. More slurry is applied to the work.

16. First candle holder is attached on top.

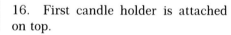
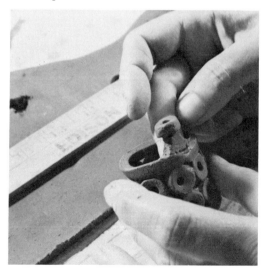

17. Four more candle holders are in place, two more will be required to complete the top.

18. The last two candle holders have been attached. This tiny candelabrum, which will hold seven small candles, is a unique and completely original design.

19. The finished piece was fired by the raku method. It is also shown in the color section alongside Irene Batt's mini-mirror.

SLAB BUILDING

A quick and simple method of making clay shapes is to roll layers of clay, cut portions, and then join them together:

PHOTO SERIES 7:   *A Slab-Built Box with Lid*

1. Rolling layers of clay is simpler and a lot less messy if we put the clay between two pieces of thin plastic (the kind used for plastic bags in which newspapers, dry cleaning, etc., are delivered), then roll with a rolling pin on top of the plastic. It is necessary to shift the position of the clay frequently so that a smooth level layer can be rolled. If a ruler is placed on either side of the clay layer to serve as a guide for the rolling pin, we are assured of a layer of even thickness.

Here is a layer of *Indian red*. A low-fire clay body has been rolled. A strip 1¼″ wide by about 8″ long has been cut. In the upper-left corner a portion of the layer is being smoothed with a potter's knife. In the lower-left corner we see a plastic container of water with a sponge in it. (Note: this is a silk sponge known as a potter's sponge. Such a sponge is more expensive than the kitchen variety, but it is much better to work with.) Above the water container we see a small glass filled with slurry; beside it sits a plastic pill bottle in a newspaper sleeve. In the extreme upper right we see a small glass, whose top is 1½″ in diameter, and a 2½″ jar lid.

2. We are going to use the glass and the jar lid as cookie cutters to cut circles out of our clay layer. A sheet of plastic wrap laid on the clay layer will allow us to cut smooth circles that will not stick to the cutters.

3. One large circle and two smaller ones have been cut through the plastic.

4. The sheet of plastic has been lifted up. The clay layer is being cut away to release the circles.

5. Trimming the edges of the circles.

6. The pill bottle in its newspaper sleeve is used as a form on which to wrap the strip of clay into a cylinder that will be the side of the box. The strip, cut to proper size and with its ends beveled, is wrapped around the bottle. Slurry is brushed on both ends of the strip.

7. The ends of the strip are welded firmly together with a potter's knife.

8. Putting on the bottom of the box. One of the small circles is inserted into the collar made by wrapping the strip around the pill bottle. Slurry is brushed into the joint. (At this point the work is still supported on the pill bottle.)

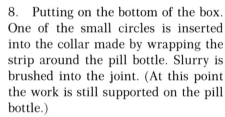

9. Smoothing the joint with the potter's knife.

10. Making a lid. Slurry is brushed on the under surface of the large circle.

11. A small circle is put in place over the slurry, then centered and pressed down firmly. This makes a flange on the underside of the lid.

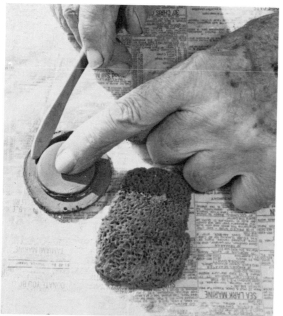

12. Forming a handle for the lid. A little strip of clay has been rolled around the point of a pencil.

13. Slurry was brushed into the end of the handle; now a ball of clay is pressed in.

14.   A depression is made in the center of the top of the lid with the modeling tool. This depression will receive the tip of the handle. Slurry is being brushed into it.

15.   Sealing the handle in place.

16.   The finished box, decorated with white slip and glazed.

PHOTO SERIES 8: *Rolling and Combining Balls of Clay—*
A Recipe Card Holder

Artist: Dorothy Shank, photos by Lee Shank

1. The artist rolls the clay in the palms of her hands, forming a ball. One side is left flat so that the object will sit firm.

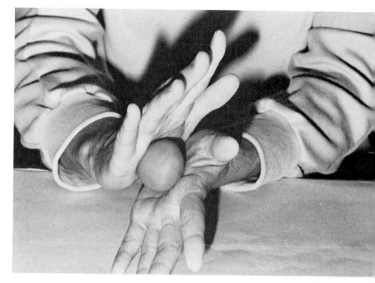

2. A wooden tool with a flat end is used to press the textured design for the back of a turtle shell into the clay.

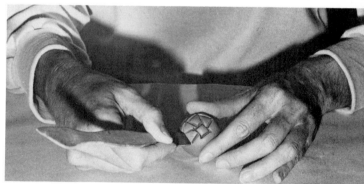

3. A small ball of clay is added for the head. A dab of slip is used to strengthen the joint.

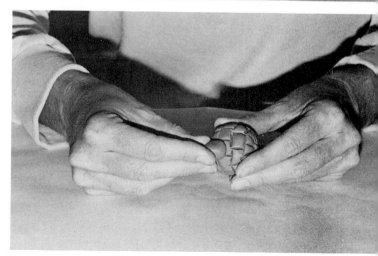

4. Feet are added to the body with slip.

5. Buttons of clay have been used for eyes. A pencil and a needle were used to shape the eyes.

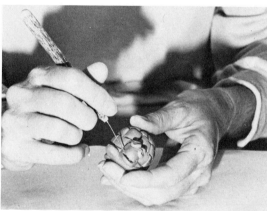

6. A needle is used to form the mouth.

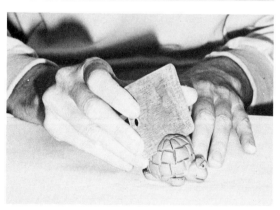

7. A piece of thin stiff plastic is pressed into the body to make a slot to hold a recipe card. The plastic is pressed in at an angle so that the card will lean back slightly.

8. Features are detailed with colored slip.

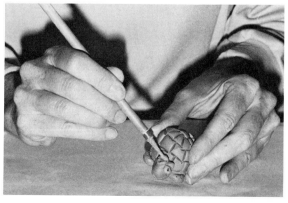

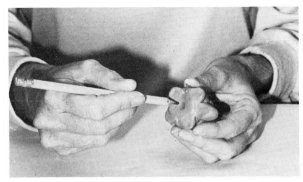

9. A pencil is used to poke a hole into the bottom; this will aid in drying and firing the little form.

10. The modeling completed. The little turtle is in the leather-hard stage with a card in place in the slot.

Note: The artist allowed for shrinkage when making the slot, and she was careful when glazing the piece to make sure that no glaze got into the slot to clog it up.

Other recipe card holders, an elephant and a lion, made by the same method, are shown in the color section.

PHOTO SERIES 9:   *Converting a Wheel-Thrown Vase into a People-Design Toothpick Holder*

Artist: Dorothy Shank, photos by Lee Shank

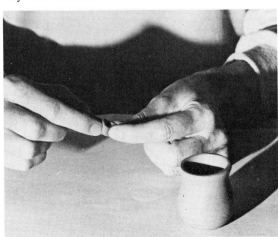

1. In the foreground is a vase 1½″ tall in the leather-hard stage. The artist is pinching a piece of clay for the nose.

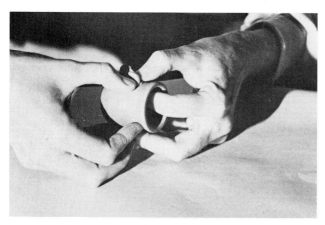

2. The nose is attached to the pot. A dab of slip is put on first.

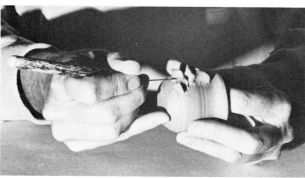

3. A coil of clay has been pressed into place and textured with a needle to form a moustache.

4. Another tiny coil of clay forms a mouth.

5. A lump of clay is put through a garlic press to form thin strings of clay that will serve as hair.

6. Hair is stuck on with a small amount of slip and pressed gently so as not to deform the hair texture.

7. Eyes are suggested with the point of a pencil.

8. A line is drawn with a pencil to separate the face from what will be the hair.

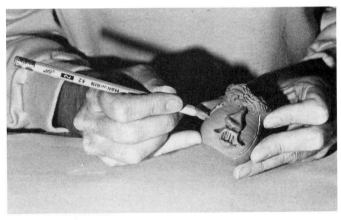

9. Applying contrasting colored slip to features.

The artist used the method of wax resist in glazing this piece: wax emulsion was brushed over the facial details that were to be left un-colored with glaze. The lower portion was waxed ¼" up from the bottom of the piece. The piece was then dipped into a brown glaze. The wax protected the face from being covered with the brown glaze (any droplets of glaze remaining over the wax were carefully wiped off). This toothpick holder and another are shown in the color section.

PINCH AND SLAB

The farmhouse shaded by a mini-tree shown in plate 2-1 was made by the slab method. (See pattern in figure 6-2.)

The garden is a pinch pot 4" x 5½" x 1" deep. The window and door openings contain bits of stained glass that were epoxied in place. The farmhouse is shown again in the color section.

PLATE 2-1

chapter · 3

THE POTTER'S WHEEL

IT USED TO BE that practically every piece of pottery other than sculpture was shaped (thrown) on a potter's wheel. Nowadays most ceramic pieces are made without a wheel, but ceramists still turn to the wheel, if only to practice their skill and to become more familiar with their clay.

Throwing on the wheel involves centering a ball of clay (which has been thoroughly wedged first) on the wheel head so that it forms a mound that turns perfectly true—that is, the turning mound has no variation in profile. Next, the mound is opened by the fingers or a tool pressing downward in the center; then the walls are raised by pressure from the fingers or tools on both the outside and the inside. In this step the wall is made thinner, the object is made taller. Next, the form is altered into an open bowl or a narrow-necked vase. As soon as it is firm enough to handle, the piece is cut free from the wheel by means of a wire and set aside to become leather hard. As soon as it is leather hard the base may be trimmed, after which it is set aside to dry until it is ready to be fired.

We must not think that throwing a tiny shape on the wheel is easier than throwing a large one—quite the contrary. The potter who hopes to throw miniature vases must first become thoroughly proficient in throwing larger shapes. There are many books which show in detail all the steps in throwing (we've written a few ourselves), but *no one ever learned to throw by reading a book*. One needs the guidance and help of a master potter and many, many hours of practice.

Vina Schemer has been a pottery instructor at the Jacksonville Art Museum for sixteen years. After giving a lesson in throwing on the potter's wheel, she sometimes cuts the piece free with a wire and removes it. This leaves a thin film of clay on the wheel head. Instead of scraping off this clay film, she works it into a tiny mound, opens it, pulls up the sides, closes the top, then opens it with the point of a pencil. The pots shown in plate 3-1 were made this way. The pot at the far left was made of Georgia red clay. The bottom was smoothed by finger.

The piece third from the left was made of high-fire porcelain. This has a series of pressed-on ball decorations. (The base of this was turned as shown in plate 3-2.) The pot with the lid is made of Georgia clay. An orangewood stick was used to make a seat for the lid.

PLATE 3-1

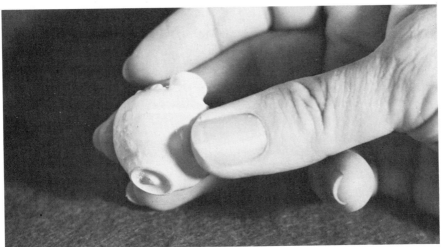

PLATE 3-2

Now let's watch Vina at work:

PHOTO SERIES 10:   *Throwing a Miniature Bowl*

1. A film of clay remaining on the wheel head is worked into a mound and opened with an orangewood stick.

2. Continuing to open.

3. The top edge has become thin and ragged, so the artist trims it off.

4. Working on the top rim.

5. Continuing to work on the rim.

6. Trimming the base.

7. Removing excess clay from the base.

8. Final touches to the rim.

9. Finished piece glazed and fired.

PHOTO SERIES 11:   *Vina Throws a Vase Shape*

1. Working a film of clay into a mound form.

2. Raising the mound.

3. Opening with a wooden tool.

4. Inserting finger.

5. Shaping.

6. Trimming the top.

7. Smoothing top.

8. More trimming on top.

9. More shaping.

10. Continuing to shape.

11. Narrowing the top.

12.   Making the top smaller.

13.   Sponging the top.

14.   Trimming the base with an up-
holstery pin.

15.   Smoothing the top with a pencil point.

16.   A lighted match is held near the top of the piece for a few seconds as the wheel turns to make the top a bit dryer and firmer.

17.   Cutting the piece free.

18. Vase is removed from the wheel.

19. Unfired vase.

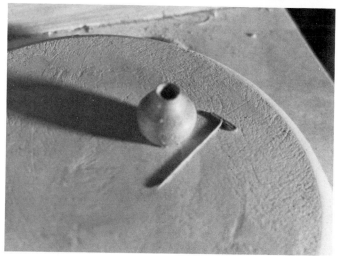

20. Finished glazed miniature vase.

THROWING FROM THE HUMP

Eleanor Madonik does not start throwing her mini-pots the way Vina Schemer does; instead, she begins with a ball of clay weighing several pounds. She centers it into a conical shape (a hump) on the wheel; then she forms a tiny pot at the apex of the cone, cuts it free with fine fishing line, lifts it off, and starts to form another shape.

PLATE 3-3

PLATE 3-4

Plate 3-3 is a close-up of a Madonik teapot. She throws the lid first, then makes a pot to fit it. The spout was also thrown on a wheel.

Plate 3-4 shows more of Eleanor's beautifully designed and decorated thrown miniature pots. A couple of mini-sculptures, including the reclining sphinx pendant, plate 3-5, got into this picture somehow—we'll say more about them in the next chapter.

PLATE 3-5

chapter 4

SKETCHING IN CLAY

Clay casts a spell that is hard to resist. Take a bit of plastic clay in your fingers, then try to put it down without altering its shape. It is not easy— you're almost certain to squeeze it or roll it, or even to start making something.

One day as we were visiting Eleanor Madonik in her studio and were talking about clay as a material, she picked up a tiny lump, and this is what happened:

PHOTO SERIES 12:   *A Fast Cat*

1.   Within less time than it takes to tell it, she formed the body and head of a little animal. A ball-point pen that happened to be lying near at hand became a modeling tool. With it she formed two ears and depressions for eyes and nostrils.

2.   Next, hind legs were squeezed.

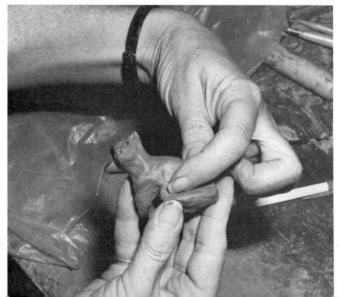

3. Front legs were modeled and the sketch was finished.

Total time involved—less than three minutes. Eleanor was not attempting a speed record; she was just having fun.

Our next visit in search of clay sketches was to the studio of Frank Eliscu.

FRANK ELISCU CREATES CLAY MINIATURES

Frank Eliscu, one of America's foremost sculptors, is known for his massive figures in stone and bronze. He is also famous for his miniature sculptures in metal. When we spoke to him about making a number of miniature figures in clay for this book, his response was enthusiastic. "You know," he said, "it's been eight years since I've held a piece of clay in my hands, but I find the idea exciting. Let's get to work."

PHOTO SERIES 13: *Warming Up*

1. The artist sketches a horse in clay.

2. He discards the horse and starts to sketch a bear.

3. Continuing the modeling.

4. Finishing the modeling.

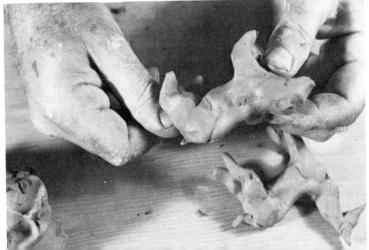

5. The bear, back view.

6. The completed bear, front view.

PHOTO SERIES 14: *A Basic Head*

1. An egg shape has been rolled out of clay. Lines have been scored to mark the center line of the face, the eyebrow line, and the line at the base of the nose.

2. A nose is added. The clay at the point of attachment was roughened and moistened first.

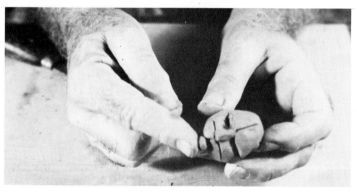

3. Depressions for eye sockets have been made; a ball of clay is added to form a chin.

4. Adding the upper lip.

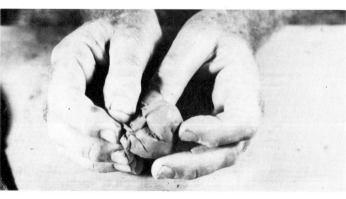

5. Modeling the upper lip.

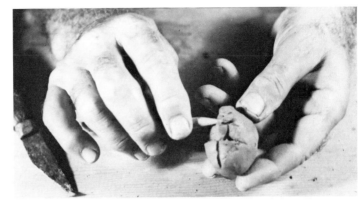

6. Adding the lower lip.

7. Small balls of clay are pressed into the eye sockets.

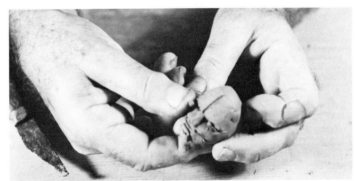

8. A tool with a round end is used to form depressions in the eyeballs (the shadows made by the depressions will give the appearance of pupils).

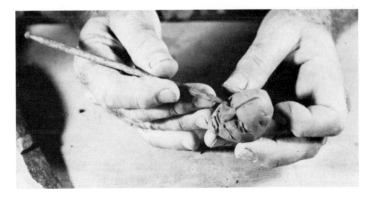

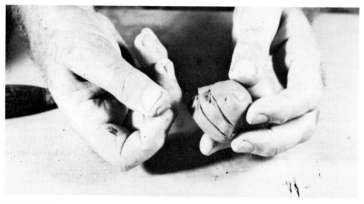

9. Forming an ear.

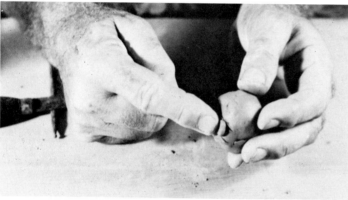

10. Attaching the ear (point of attachment is roughened and moistened to secure ear).

11. Tiny strips of clay have been rolled to form the hair. These are attached to the head.

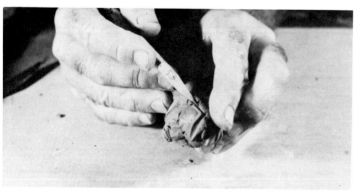

12. Shaping the hair.

13. The completed head. Note: except for the modeling tool with a rounded end, a pencil, and a knife, all of the shaping was done by the artist's fingers.

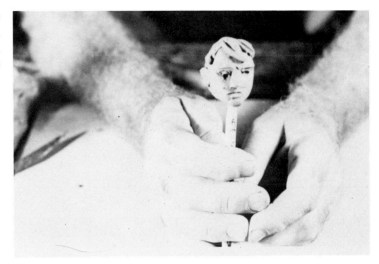

PHOTO SERIES 15:   *A Kneeling Prophet*

1. A basic head has been modeled. Small bits of clay have been rolled to form hair and beard.

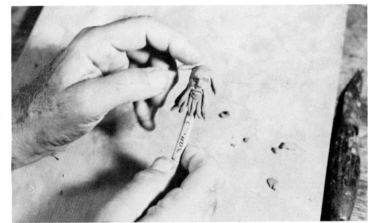

2. A strip of clay is cut for the body.

3. The head has been added to the body. The body is bent at the knees.

4. Clay to form the garment drapery is attached.

5. Arms are added.

6. A pencil is used to model drapery.

7. The right hand has been inserted into its sleeve. A hole has been made in the left sleeve to receive the left hand, fingers of which are being formed.

8. The completed figurine.

64

PHOTO SERIES 16:   *Two Herons*

1. A tapered cylinder has been rolled.

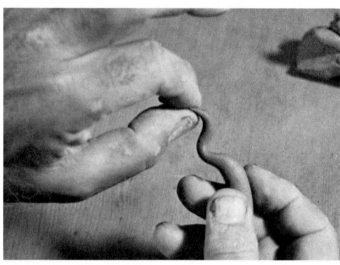

2. The thinner end is then bent to form a neck.

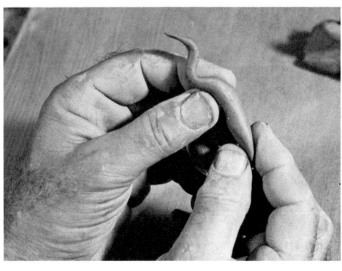

3. The tail is formed by gently pulling on the other end of the cylinder.

4. Tiny balls of clay are added to form the feathers; each ball is pinched between the fingers as it is added.

5. A ball of clay is attached to make the shoulders.

6. Forming and shaping the feathers.

7.   The second bird is formed. The first bird rests on a lump of clay.

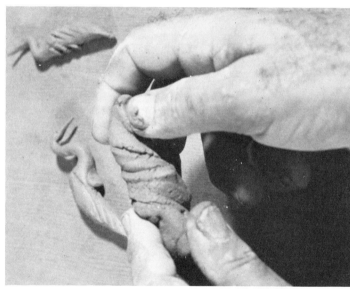

8.   Twisting a tree stump.

9.   The first bird is placed on the twisted stump.

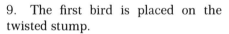
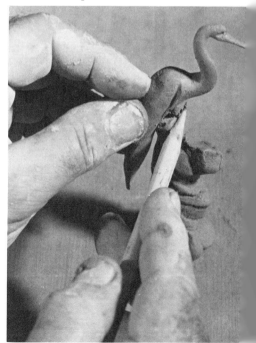

10.   The second bird perches on the stump.

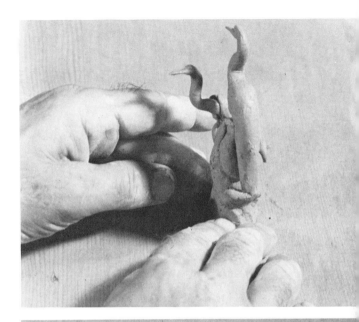

11.   Altering the positions of the birds for better design.

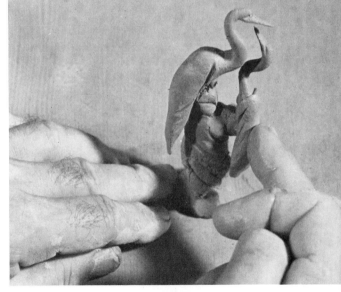

12.   Fern fronds are modeled and attached to the twisted tree stump (point of attachment is roughened and moistened to secure the fronds).

13. The completed figurine. The fired and glazed figurine is also shown in the color section.

Note: The two birds do not touch each other; if they did touch, there would be a strong likelihood that the point of contact would break during firing.

PHOTO SERIES 17: *A Nude Figure*

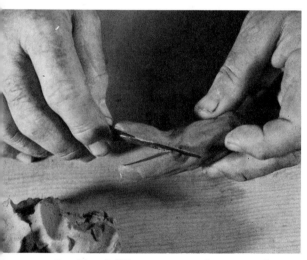

1. Frank Eliscu starts with a strip of clay. He makes a cut to start the formation of two legs.

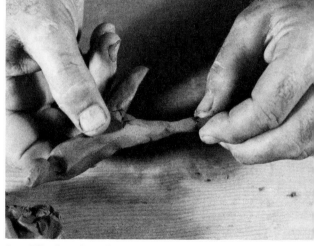

2. The head and neck were formed by pinching the end of the strip of clay—legs are being modeled.

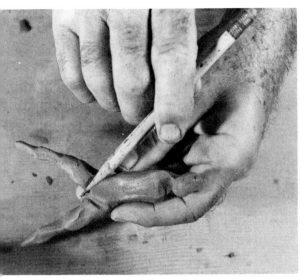

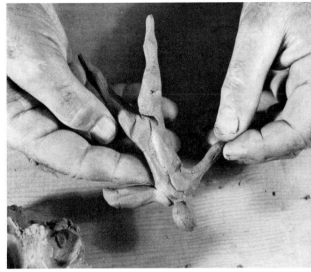

3. A pencil is used to form definition between legs and torso.

4. Arms are attached.

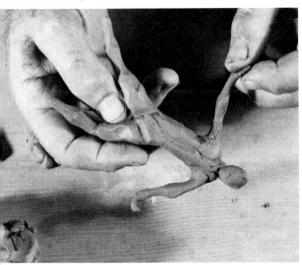

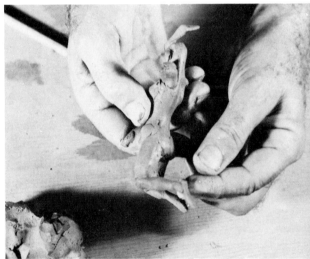

Arms are being modeled.

6. The figure will kneel. A piece of clay is put in back of the knees to serve as a temporary support.

7. Hair has been added. Arms are folded over the head. Details of anatomy are refined.

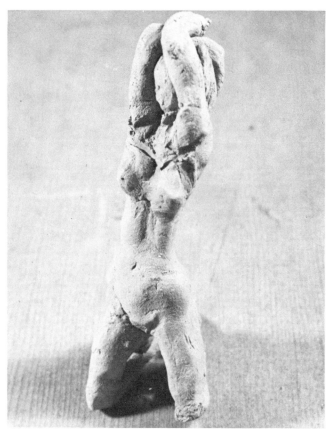

8. The modeling completed. The figure is now firm enough to stand without the support, so the lump of clay is removed from the back of the knees.

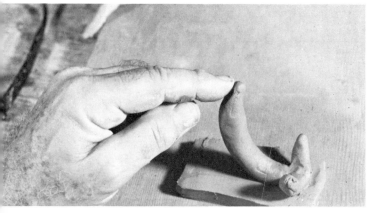

PHOTO SERIES 18: *A Fox*

1. Frank Eliscu starts with a small rectangular base of clay. A cigar shape is being attached to form the body and the neck. Two small cigar-shaped portions have been put in place to form the hind legs.

2. The head has been formed and is being attached. Depressions have been made for the eye sockets. Sides of the head have been pinched out to form whiskers.

3. Tiny balls of clay have been inserted in the eye sockets, whiskers have been scored. The ears are being modeled. Note that a lump of clay serves as a temporary support for the body of the fox.

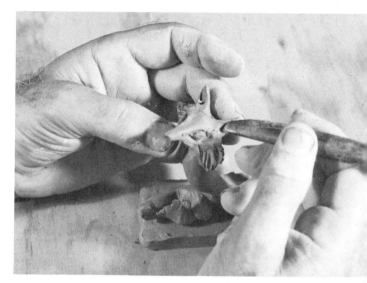

4. A tail is added.

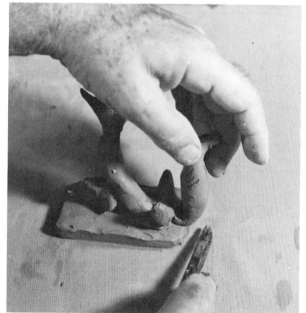

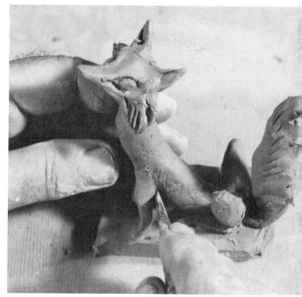

5. The tail has been ruffled with a pointed tool. Two front legs are attached.

6. The modeling has been completed.

7. Another view. The fired and glazed figurine is also shown in the color section.

THE GROUP

In plate 4-1 the six miniature creations are drying in afternoon sunlight. Each of these tiny sculptures took Frank Eliscu less than half an hour to make.

It is obvious that the clay must be kept moist and plastic during the modeling of a figurine, but Eliscu works so rapidly that only twice did he have to use an atomizer to spray the figures (the nude and the birds).

Next day (plate 4-2). Eliscu has no kiln, so we had to bring the dried figurines home with us to be fired and glazed (a distance of 220 miles). To transport such delicate objects that far, it was necessary to pack them very specially. The figures were placed on a piece of corrugated cardboard and outlines of their positions were traced. Then flat-headed nails were driven through the cardboard from the underside so that the tiny pieces could be held firmly by the nails that projected up from the floor on which they would rest.

As shown in this photograph, the fox is held in place by four nails and so are the bear and the prophet. One nail was sufficient for the head and also for the birds. Two nails held the nude. The ride was over some bumpy roads—but all passengers arrived safely.

PLATE 4-1

PLATE 4-2

chapter 5

PLAYTHINGS

SOME of the oldest ceramics that have survived to delight us are toys—playthings not only for children but even for grown-ups.

The color section shows pictures of some contemporary ceramic toys from Mexico; among them are a couple of whistles. These are low-fired earthenware.

Vina Schemer makes toys for Christmas trees. Plate 5-1 shows the head of an elf; 1½″ tall, made of high-fired porcelain. This was thrown on a potter's wheel—the top was pulled up into a long narrow shape that was curled over to form a hat. Then eyes, nose, and ears were stuck on. The loop of the hat makes it easy to hang Mr. Elf on a tree branch.

Vina made many dozens of these at the rate of four or five an hour. All of them were snapped up by appreciative collectors.

The following Christmas, Vina made *critters* (see color section), imaginary animals that have curly manes from which they can be hung on the tree. But these critters have a special feature—they are whistles. She told us there must be a closed space so constructed that air blown into the chamber through an opening is split by a projecting edge; this makes the whistling sound. To make the explanation clearer, she drew this diagram for us (figure 5-A).

PLATE 5-1

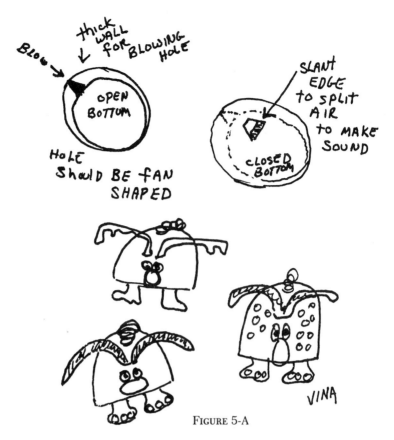

FIGURE 5-A

Vina's Christmas ornaments have become very popular. Collectors wait with anticipation to see what next year's creations will be.

MEXICAN MINIATURES

During the nine years that we lived in Mexico we were able to collect some fascinating toys made by native Mexican artists. (This seems redundant; we have never met a native Mexican who was *not* an artist.) Mexicans seem to be born with a sense of design: the first concern of the vendors of fruits or vegetables at a market or at a roadside stand is arranging their wares in attractive geometric patterns.

Mexican villages far from big cities do not have toy stores, but the children are not neglected. Their parents make toys for them, using all sorts of materials that happen to be available—straw, wood, stone, tin cans, and, of course, clay. Children often work along with their elders, helping to make toys that will be carried to market and sold.

Let's take a look at some of our treasures. In plate 5-2 is a tiny kitchen in a shadow box, 6½" x 5½" x 1½" deep. The pitchers, the plates, the casseroles, all are made to the scale 1" = 1'. In the foreground a rolling pin is ready to roll dough for *pan dulces* (sugar cookies), and in the lower left corner is a griddle on which cookies are being cooked. This

PLATE 5-2

PLATE 5-4

PLATE 5-3

miniature kitchen was probably made for a little girl who could show it to her doll and command, "Cocinar!" The woman who sold it to us might very well have been that little girl grown up.

In plate 5-3 an acrobat balances on his chin on the top of a pole on which he twirls. The pole is 4″ high; the acrobat measures 2½″ in length. At left is a rather odd merry-go-round on which the passengers seem to be hanging by their hair. (The little figures really hang on wire loops.) These two pieces are made of clay, fired and then painted brilliant colors.

PLATE 5-5

PLATE 5-6

The mermaid in plate 5-4 was cast in a drain mold, then fired and painted in brilliant colors. She is ¾″ tall.

Plate 5-5 shows a six-animal orchestra modeled in a buff clay, fired not glazed. The figures are about 1½″ tall, more or less. Animal musicians of this design are popular in Mexico; some families have been making them for generations. The woman who sold us these tiny figures told us that they had been made by her ten-year-old daughter.

A serpent comes to Eden in plate 5-6. It is built of clay, fired, and then painted with aniline dyes mixed with egg white. The leaves of the tree are shades of cerise, hot purple, vivid greens, and orange. The serpent's tongue is vermillion. Base of tree to top of bird measures 5½″; Adam and Eve are each 2½″ tall.

The tiny china tea set on a tray in plate 5-7 is made of red clay; the pieces and the tray were thrown on the wheel and then fired and waxed. The teapot measures 2¾″ from handle to tip of spout.

Plate 5-8 shows an interesting figure of a woman holding a bird. (Could this be a Mexican Leda?) The three pots at her feet were wheel thrown. The woman too was shaped on a wheel, then arms, head shawl, features, and ornaments were added. She is 5″ tall, made of buff clay, fired but not glazed.

The two horses in plate 5-9 are whistles. Each horse is 3″ tall. They are shown again in the color section along with two whistle critters made by Vina Schemer.

Plate 5-10 reveals a truly mysterious piece of work; it was made in the southern part of Mexico. The cup, 2¾″ tall, has emerging from it the head, arms, and legs of what seems to be a demon with goatlike features

PLATE 5-7

PLATE 5-9

PLATE 5-8

and horns. He holds in his arms a horse 1¾" long. At the top of the picture we see two projections; these are the ears of a fox-headed figure who is munching a chicken. Could it be that the goat is going to eat that tiny horse?

Plates 5-11 and 5-12 show two views of a delightful clay doll figure, 7" tall. She was shaped on a wheel; then arms, features, hair, and ornaments were pressed on. The girl is patting a tortilla between her hands (the traditional way of making tortillas). Attached to a pedestal in front of her is a *metate*, a flat stone, on which she has ground the corn to make the dough for the tortilla.

PLATE 5-10   PLATE 5-11   PLATE 5-12

There is a special ceremony connected with this figure. When the child who owns the doll becomes fifteen years of age, there is a party at which she and the girls who are her playmates promenade in a circle, the fifteen-year-old holding the doll on top of her head. At the end of the promenade she puts the doll away to keep for the little girl she will have later when she marries. She is now a woman and no longer plays with dolls.

In plate 5-13 we see some really mini-miniatures, brilliantly decorated. At the left is a hen with two of her chicks; she is ⅜″ tall. The piggy bank next to her is less than ½″ long from point of snout to curl of tail Believe it or not, this little bank is hollow and has a slot for depositing coins. The burro is ¾″ long. The woman paddling a boat laden with flowers on Lake Xochimilco is ⅝″ tall, and her boat measures 1″ from stem to stern. Each of the two birds guarding their nest with eggs in it is ½″ long. What a labor of love it must have been to fashion these tiny gems, so colorful and so perfect in detail!

The postman in plate 5-14 is 5″ tall, as are the musicians in plate 5-15 and the wood seller and the pottery vendor in plate 5-16. These figurines were modeled in clay, fired, and painted—except the musicians, which were glazed.

Plate 5-17 shows two owls, 1½″ tall, one of whom is turning his back to us. These are examples of *Jalisco ware*, high-fired porcelain with overglaze painting. The Jalisco artists are masters of the delicate brush. Other examples of Jalisco ware are shown in the color section.

The candlesticks in plate 5-18 are each 2½″ tall. If you look closely you will see a tiny bird perched on the base of the one to the left. The one to the right has three owls perched on it; each owl is ⅜″ tall.

Brightly colored Christmas ornaments from ½″ to 1½″ in height are

PLATE 5-13

PLATE 5-14

PLATE 5-15

PLATE 5-16

shown in plate 5-19. Some more Christmas tree ornaments are shown in the color section.

In plate 5-20 our visit to a Mexican mini-world ends with a serenade by a mariachi trio, 1½″ tall.

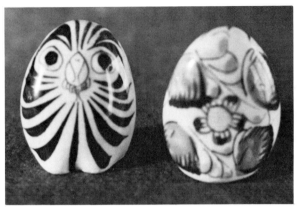

PLATE 5-17

PLATE 5-18

PLATE 5-19

PLATE 5-20

The next time you visit Mexico pay a visit to the National Museum of Popular Art in downtown Mexico City where there are exhibits of the work of craftsmen from all parts of Mexico. Objects on display show good design in straw, glass, wood, leather, and ceramics. One section is devoted to a display of miniatures, all less than 1″ tall. The minute detail of the figures is amazing: there are men and women performing their daily tasks; bullfighters displaying their skills in *corridas de toros* in an arena before an audience of hundreds; a circus with clowns, acrobats, trapeze artists. Outstanding among the artists creating these miniatures is Angel Carranza, a man well into his eighties who has been making miniatures since he was twelve years old.

The 5″ tall figures shown in plates 5-21 and 5-22 were made in South America. The man has been carrying a bundle of wood, now he is tired so he sits down to massage his foot. The woman is tasting the soup she is preparing. These figurines are from the collection of Srta. Maria Laura Aviña G.

From Central America come the two whimsical miniature creations in plate 5-23. Two hens sit brooding on platform discs. When the hens are lifted up, they reveal a vendor of fruit and vegetables (left) and a woman selling gourds, who has a little dog and a chicken beside her. Both figurines are ¾″ tall.

PLATE 5-21   PLATE 5-22

PLATE 5-23

Bits of whimsey of this type are quite popular in Central America. We have seen many of the same size—one in which the little hen covered a woman cooking her dinner on a kitchen stove, complete with chimney, and another in which a man was selling plates—his wares were spread before him, each plate intricately painted with a different design.

FOUNTAINS

Carl Milles, the great Scandinavian sculptor, created one of the finest and biggest (second only in size to Mt. Rushmore) sculptural compositions in the world, the multiple-figure fountain *Meeting of the Waters,* in St. Louis, Missouri. He referred to it as a "water toy for grown-ups."

We set out to make two of the smallest fountains in the world, the two shown in the color section. These are tabletop water toys.

Fountains are fascinating projects (plates 5-24 and 5-25); the problem is getting pumps to fit them. Our advice: buy a pump first; then build a fountain around it.

Plate 5-26 shows the pump that operates the park fountain. This pump can be plugged into regular household current. See figure 5-1 on page 86. The pump for the mermaid fountain operates on DC and as shown in plate 5-27 requires a transformer. The transformer creates a space problem, and if the tiny 15-volt pump is run steadily for several hours, it will overheat and soon burn out, hence we do not recommend this type of pump.

Making this fountain was fun and we plan to keep the mermaid and her spouting fish, but we will build another bowl for her that will accommodate a tiny submersible pump.

PLATE 5-24

PLATE 5-25

PLATE 5-26

PLATE 5-27

Figure 5-1

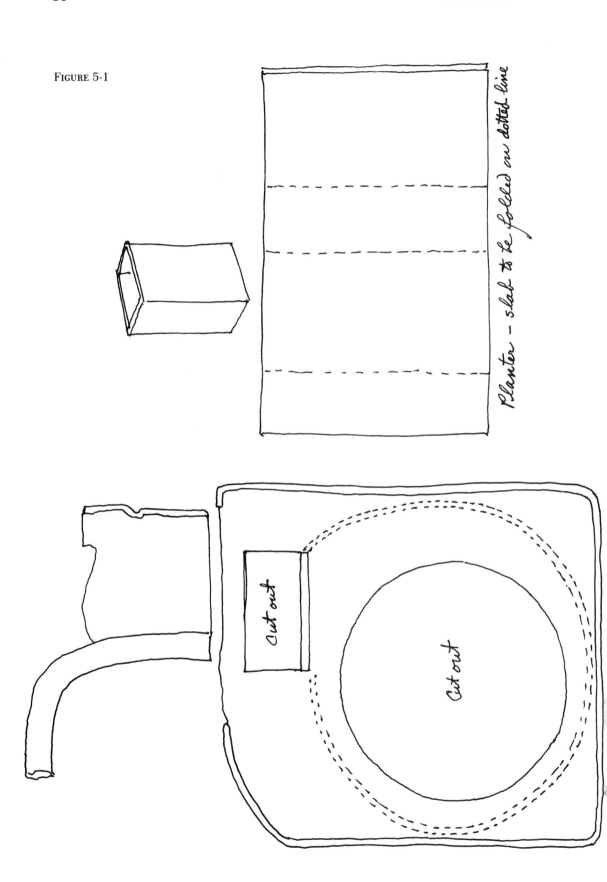

Planter – slab to be folded on dotted line

Cut out

Cut out

We like making fountains; over the past years we have made (and written about) quite a few. Figures 5-2, 5-3, 5-4, and 5-5 show some drawings by Carla. Here are the two little pumps that are submersible and work on house current (see figures 5-6 and 5-7).

Fountains are a real challenge to one's inventiveness, so—get out your sketchbook and jot down some ideas.

Cut four slats

FIGURE 5-2

Cut two bench forms. Be sure to make the openings wide enough to allow the slats to slip into place. Do the trimming and fitting during the leather hard stage.

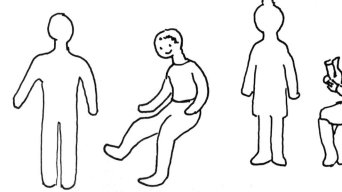

These may be cut out of a slab of clay — then pinched, squeezed and bent into the desired final form — or little coils and balls of clay can be rolled, scored, and finally formed to resemble these.

For the Park fountain

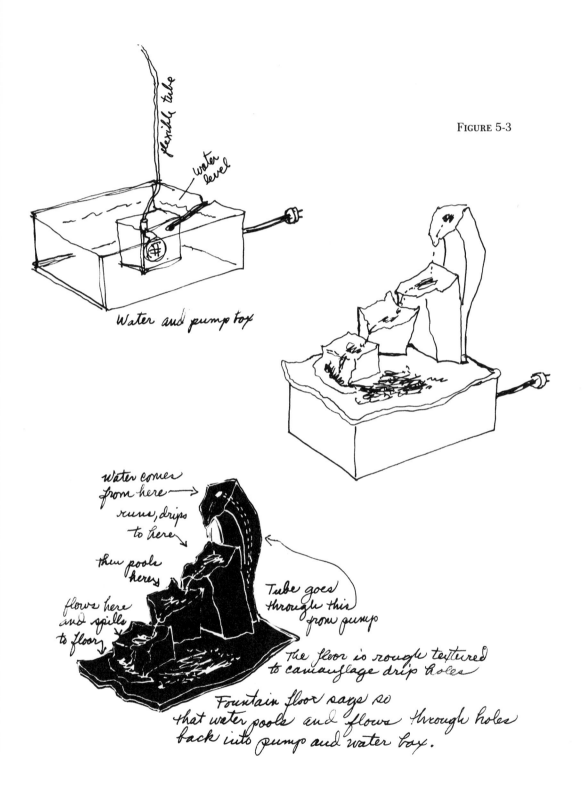

FIGURE 5-3

flexible tube

water level

Water and pump box

water comes
from here →
runs, drips
to here →
then pools
here →
flows here
and spills
to floor →

Tube goes
through this
from pump

The floor is rough textured
to camouflage drip holes

Fountain floor sags so
that water pools and flows through holes
back into pump and water box.

FIGURE 5-4

Base of design must
sag and slope inward
so that water will flow
through inconspicuous
openings at foot of
plant design — thus
returning all water back
to pump — water box.

Plant fronds of clay are very
thin except area surrounding
thin plastic tube carrying water
up from pump in water box.
Pump dealer or aquarian supplier
can sell you the connection that
will carry three tiny tubes for
water from the one main tube.

Tiny tube carries water
to top of umbrella through
the girl's left leg then from
stem next to her shoulder.

Bowl with umbrella girl can
be lifted from pump and
water box. Water returns
slowly to pump box through
opening in "floor" opposite the
cord outlet.

FIGURE 5-5

Pool and pump box.
A "table" with two fountain holes
sits over pump.

A 'T' connection is attached
to pump so that two streams
of water are pumped out to
form a double fountain.
This may be purchased from an
aquarium supplier.

The plants and
trees are of ceramic.
The entire form on its
base may be lifted
off of the fountain pool.

gold colored glass is
adhered to back of building
to give a golden glow
through cut out openings.

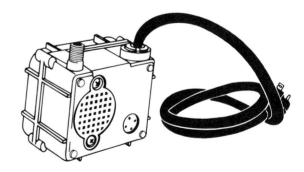

FIGURE 5-6. Little Giant I-MA   FIGURE 5-7. Little Giant P-AAA

chapter 6

MINIATURE SCENES

NOW WE COME to one of the most thrilling areas of mini-ceramics: we will build houses and plant gardens and create tiny people to enjoy them.

DREAM CASTLES

When we saw a photo of Chris Clark with one of her castles in *Ceramics Monthly*, we *had* to write and ask her to tell us more. Her reply was generous—filled with philosophical thoughts about how she loves to create mini-castles complete with moats and dungeons and secret passageways through which one's mind may wander as in a dream world.

She sent some photos too. Plate 6-1 (photo by Lee Milne) pictures a porcelain castle small enough to fit into a 3″ x 3″ x 6″ cone box. On the back of the photo Chris noted that it had a transparent glaze over all, with adobe glaze on the roofs.

We wondered about *adobe glaze*—had never heard the term before— so we telephoned Chris in Denver to ask about it. Turns out that adobe glaze is a clay used to make bricks. Chris just digs it from a hill where the brickmakers get it. All she has to do is add water. (More about using glaze in chapter 11.)

The stoneware castle in plate 6-2 (photo by Ed Arrowood) is a candle holder, 15″ tall. The tower tops show effective use of the wax-resist method of decoration (described in chapter 13). Note that the shutters can be opened and closed.

Plate 6-3 (photo by Lee Milne) shows another castle made of porcelain, glazed over all with clear glaze, with adobe glaze on the turrets; it measures 15″ x 7″ x 7″.

PLATE 6-1

PLATE 6-2

PLATE 6-3

PLATE 6-4

A planted desert garden with a castle in the middle of it is shown in plate 6-4 (photo by Ed Arrowood). If you look closely, you'll see that a dragon guards the portal. This piece measures 10″ x 7″ x 7″.

Ever hear of a chess set in which, except for the knights, all of the pieces had castle turrets? Plate 6-5 (photo by Lee Milne) shows another of Chris Clark's creations. The white pieces are made of porcelain and the black pieces are made of stoneware. The board is 9″ x 9″ x 2″.

PLATE 6-5

A NEW YORK BROWNSTONE

Sometimes an idea can be created directly in clay without previous experimentation, but there are times when an idea is better carried out if a mock-up is made out of paper or cardboard, especially if the work is architectural. For the brownstone house the idea was easily formulated: first a sketch was made; then it was transferred to cardboard as a flat pattern. In this case an English-muffin carton was ideal because it was manageable and its wax coating was protective so that it could be used more than once if the artist wished to do a variation on the design. See figure 6-1.

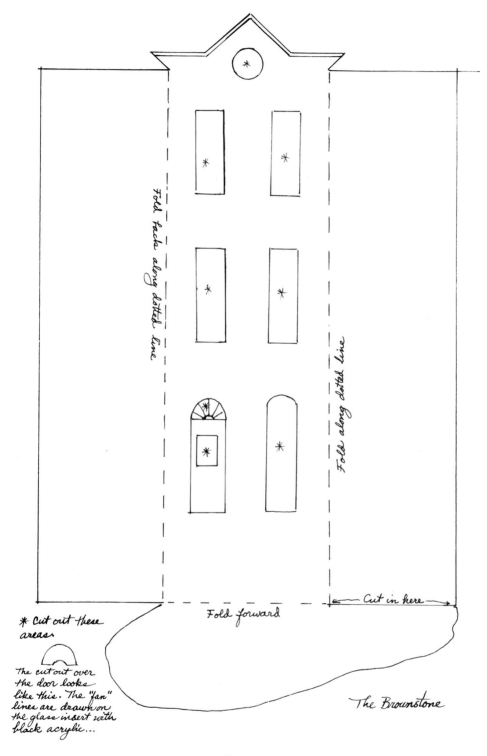

Fold back along dotted line

Fold along dotted line

Cut in here

Fold forward

* Cut out these
areas.

The cut out over
the door looks
like this. The "fan"
lines are drawn on
the glass insert with
black acrylic...

The Brownstone

FIGURE 6-1

PHOTO SERIES 19

1. A slab of clay was rolled large enough to accommodate the cardboard pattern (overall dimensions of the pattern are 11″ x 8½″).

The clay was in excellent working condition, so a thin sheet of clear plastic (the kind the morning newspaper is delivered in) was placed over the clay as the rolling was done. When the slab was the right size, the plastic was removed, the pattern placed on the clay slab, then the plastic laid on top of the pattern and the rolling pin was rolled over all once more. (As even thickness is important in a slab-built piece, two wooden slats were used at each side of the clay to support the ends of the rolling pin.)

Rolling the pattern on top of the clay imprinted the pattern (the cutout windows and door). The plastic sheet was then removed and cutting around the pattern was done with a potter's knife. Here, a cut is being made to separate the side of the building from the sidewalk. The cut terminated where the knife is in the picture.

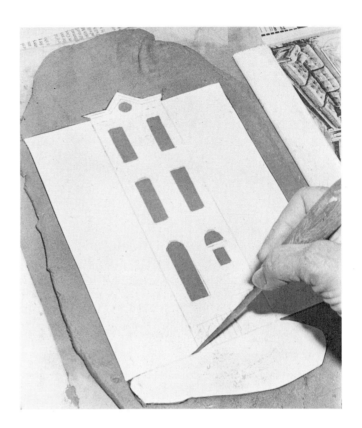

2. The pattern is carefully lifted from the clay.

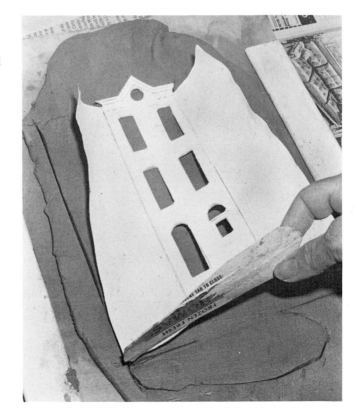

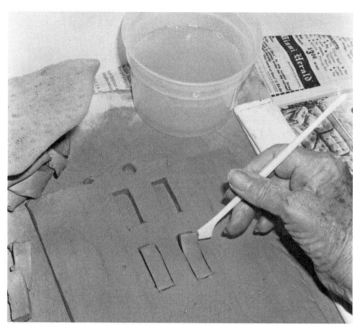

3. The excess clay has been removed from the outer edges of the design. The dampened sponge in the upper left is used to keep excess clay moist and workable for additions to be made later. The container of water is kept at hand to moisten the pottery tools while work is in progress and also to keep the tools clean. The windows are being cut out and removed with a modeling tool that has a flat end.

4. Here we see the house wrapped around a wooden block that has a sleeve of newspaper around it. The stairs have been formed and put in place as have the coils that form the railings.

5. The building draped on the wooden block is tilted back and is resting on several blocks of wood as support. This angle makes it easier to work. Narrow strips of clay have been placed to form the eaves. Now, rectangles of clay have been cut from a small slab and are being attached to form windowsills. Each bit of clay is put into place with slurry. Small cubes of clay are then placed under the sills as supports.

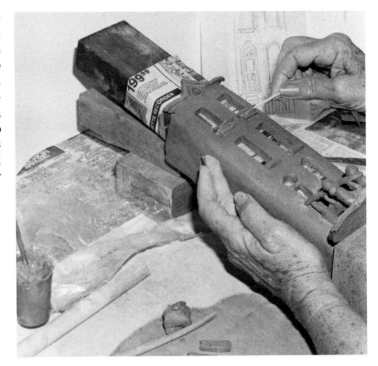

6. The window frames and doorframe have been cut and placed. The parlor window frame is being cut to match the doorframe. In the left foreground is a dowel stick—this is used for rolling small slabs of clay when work is in progress and the work area is too small for the regular rolling pin. Note the plastic just beyond the sponge; all rolling is done with the plastic sheet over the clay.

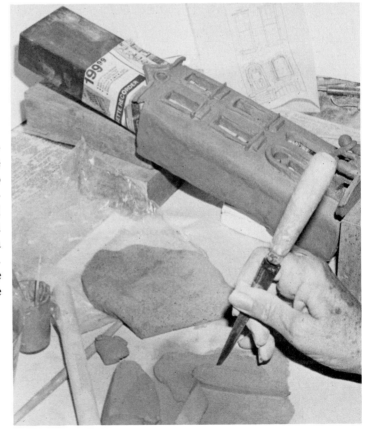

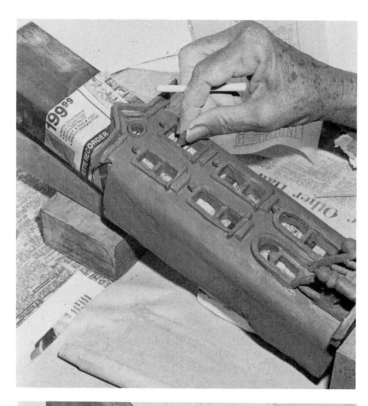

7.   Here a measured rectangle of clay is being put into the window to form the sash. Notice the little coils in place as ornaments over the windows.

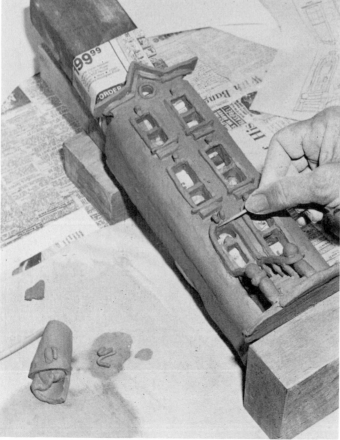

8.   The ornament over the door, a double coil, is being secured with the point of a toothpick (rounded wooden toothpicks are handy tools for the miniaturist). Ornaments under the eaves were added in the same fashion—they were made of tiny cubes of clay incised with the toothpick.

9. The garden is a pinch pot that has a protected area for the light fixture. In this picture we see it ready to receive the house, which has been fired. Glass has been glued with epoxy to the back side of the windows and the door. The parlor window has a piece of lace glued to it, and the window with green glass in it has been painted with white acrylic stripes.

10. Front view of the finished house sitting in its garden. There is a tiny pussycat on the sill of the second-floor window. The house with interior light is shown in the color section.

11. Detail showing pussycat who has the run of the house because he can sit on any windowsill, the steps, or in the garden.

PINCH POT REAL ESTATE

In plates 6-6 and 6-7 we see the type of dish that is used to hold the lot on which the brownstone house shown in Photo Series 19 stands. This is actually a pinch pot made freehand with a hole in the bottom to permit wires to enter from below. A collar of clay fastened above the hole protects the wires when the plants in the garden are watered. In plate 6-7 we see the electrical fixtures needed. The smaller socket (center) has a cardboard sleeve to protect it.

A similar dish made the same way, but considerably smaller, holds the farmhouse shown in the color section.

Plate 6-6

Plate 6-7

Before making a building lot out of clay, decide what kinds of plants you intend to use so that your pinch pot will be deep enough for the roots. For instance, the tree planted near the park fountain shown in the color section has a planting area 5½″ deep. See figure 6-2.

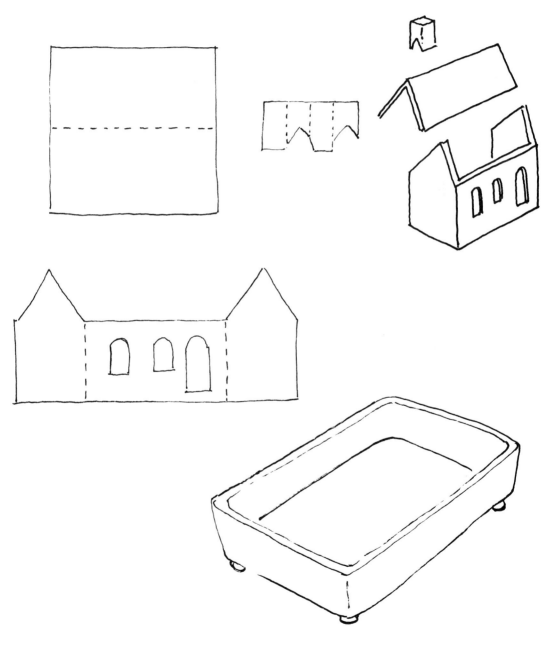

FIGURE 6-2

AN ANTIQUE SHOP

This charming antique shop caught our fancy one day as we passed it. We returned, made a sketch, and decided that one day it would be fun to create it in clay. A cardboard pattern was made from the sketch in the same manner as the New York brownstone in Photo Series 19. See figure 6-3.

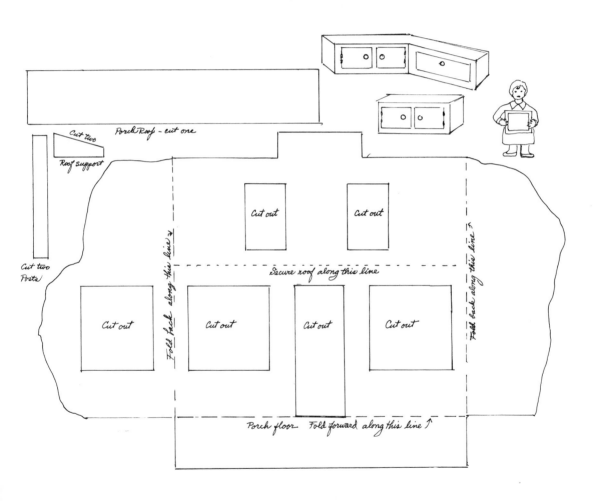

FIGURE 6-3

PHOTO SERIES 20

1. This shows the assembly of the pieces that were rolled in clay, cut, folded, and built into the shape of a store with a false front. There had to be a lot of temporary props made of clay to support the porch roof until the supporting posts were strong enough to hold it.

2. This shows a view of the inside of the store. Window storage cupboards have been put in place. These were hollowed-out blocks of clay, and they gave an extra solidity to the standing structure. In this picture we see some of the merchandise that might be offered for sale. (Do you recognize some of the pots we made back in chapter 1?)

3. The finished shop. The figure in the side window was cut from a clay slab (in the real shop this figure is cut out of a large board). The message "Open 10–5" was scratched through the glaze on the blackboard before firing (sgraffito).

The shop needed two firings, the first for Majolica glazing and the second firing for the red glaze on the posts and window trim, and for the metallic glazes used on the porch roof and floor. The cutout figure has been glued into place with epoxy.

The miniature ware displayed can be changed from time to time, nothing is glued in place. The pieces shown on the wall in picture 2 are stuck on with Mini-Hold (a clear wax) purchased from a hobby shop for miniaturists. Mini-hold is a handy thing to have; it will hold a piece firmly to a wall, but you can pull it off with ease and it leaves no mark on the object or the wall.

LOOKING BACK

Here are three pictures showing the work of Sandra McKenzie Schmitt. This artist has skillfully captured the feeling of a way of life that hardly exists anymore—the front porches, gables, and cupolas of farmhouses and the friendliness of small towns. The plasticity of Sandra's clay and the dexterity of her fingers and her mind beautifully depict the gingerbread qualities of these structures.

Plate 6-8: "My Grandmother's House." The house is 8″ tall and made of buff stoneware fired to cone 6.

Plate 6-9: "Square Victorian." This house is 9″ tall and is also made of buff stoneware fired to cone 6.

PLATE 6-8   PLATE 6-9

PLATE 6-10

Plate 6-10: "The Wedding." This charming bit of village scenery, measuring 18" x 20" x 10", shows houses and a church grouped around a village square boasting park benches and a piece of statuary. The bride and groom are seen coming out of the church door. This is made of red clay fired to cone 6.

CERAMICS FOR DOLLHOUSES

All of the miniature porcelains shown in plates 6-11 through 6-17 are the work of Dee Snyder, an avid collector of fine porcelains. In her travels

PLATE 6-11

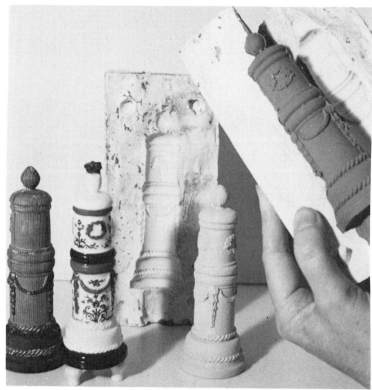

PLATE 6-12

PLATE 6-13

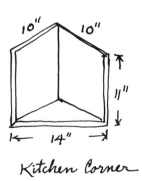

Kitchen Corner

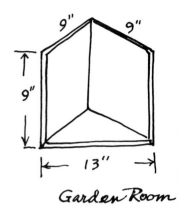

Garden Room

PLATE 6-14

PLATE 6-15

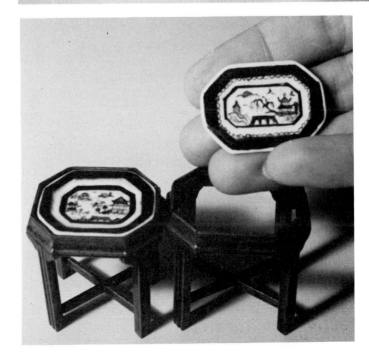

PLATE 6-16

PLATE 6-17

she has collected exquisite pieces of Delft, Sèvres, faience, and Chinese export porcelain ware. Some of these she has produced in miniature for dollhouses and for dollhouse rooms. She also created many original designs for continental porcelain stoves and other dollhouse accessories.

Dee is a talented artist and a fine craftsperson. Many of her miniature objects are made by using molds (molds she makes herself). She is adept at combining bits of jewelry, decorative-cord trim, beads, and similar bits of tiny ornamentation to create constructions from which her molds can be cast.

In plate 6-11 the piece at the left is an antique toothpick holder shown upside down. This will serve as the baseof an ornamental stove. Second from the left is a casting made from a mold of the toothpick holder. In the center is a casting of the stove top made from the piece right of center: plastiline was used to adhere jewelry findings to the sides of a child's alphabet block; the top section is a piece of brass ornament from a lamp and on top of that was added a finial; these were stuck together with plastiline and additions to the design were carved into the plastiline. The entire piece was then sized and a three-piece mold was made. At the far right is a stove combining the center casting with the cast of the toothpick holder. The units were epoxied together after they were glazed and fired.

Plate 6-12 is another continental stove by Dee. The shape at the far left is a piece of wood turned on a lathe by the artist's husband, Brandt, also a fine craftsman. Ornaments were modeled on with clay; then the whole thing was sized and a three-piece mold was cast. At the far right is a casting being removed from the mold. A casting that has been dried and trimmed but not fired (called greenware at this stage) is shown in the center of the picture. Second from the left we see a finished, glazed, and decorated stove, 6″ tall. Note the top section is different from that of the casting. Dee frequently makes alterations on portions of the castings while they are still moist (before they become leather hard). Feet were made and glazed, then applied separately with epoxy.

Plate 6-13: "Kitchen Corner." The cook is 5″ tall, made from a Seely doll mold, then dressed by Dee. The dog is 1¾″ tall.

Plate 6-14: "Garden Room." The leopard is 2½″ tall.

Plate 6-15 displays miniature porcelain tableware. Front row, left to right: Imari plate, Williamsburg plate with cuckoo pattern, Canton platter, Chinese ginger jar. Back row, left to right: Old English spirit barrel, faience tureen, and in the hand—a plum brandy barrel.

Plate 6-16 presents a pair of Charleston platter tables. Canton platters by Dee. Tables by Don Ward.

In plate 6-17 the seventeenth-century Dutch Porseleinkamer (also shown in color section) is modeled after a room in the Rijksmuseum in Amsterdam. It is 11″ high and 13″ wide.

LITTLE PEOPLE FOR DOLLHOUSES

Tiny figures may, of course, be modeled freehand, but dollhouse enthusiasts usually demand a more realistic representation than is obtainable from simple hand modeling. For them there is a large source of supply of all kinds of people—babies, children, and grown-ups—that can be bought precast in molds. For those who wish to make their own castings, literally hundreds of different molds are available.

Jane Hernandez's *Little People* (plate 6-18) are made of porcelain. Jane uses commercial molds, then makes alterations to the castings while they are still moist. Four babies in this picture are made from the same mold: the one with diaper only and large booties was dipped in colored porcelain slip to make the diaper and the booties. The hair is brown porcelain painted on while the casting was wet. The baby in the playsuit (lower left) had hair, features, and clothing painted by the china-painting method. The black baby, also from the same mold, had features changed while the casting was wet and black porcelain hair painted on the wet casting.

Plate 6-18

Making miniature dolls has become a big industry. Jane Hernandez now has a new dollhouse family in production and has all the orders that she can fill. Jane suggests that any people interested in tiny characters for dollhouses would enjoy a visit to the Dollhouse and Toy Museum in Chevy Chase, Maryland.

DOLLHOUSE TABLEWARE

Plates 6-19 through 6-22 show the work of Evelyn Strid, a newcomer to the world of ceramics (see chapter 14). Evelyn does not use molds but makes all her pieces freehand, to the scale of $1'' = 1'$.

In plate 6-19 the artist trims some greenware. One of the pieces has been decorated with one-stroke underglaze.

Plate 6-20 shows reproductions of Chinese Rose Medallion ware.

Plate 6-19

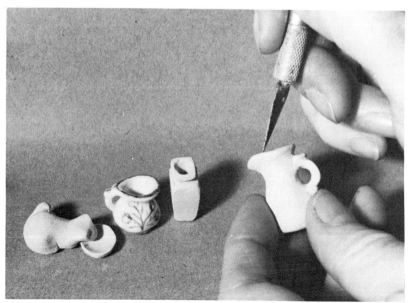

PLATE 6-20

PLATE 6-21

PLATE 6-22

In plate 6-21 the penny at the right gives you an idea of the size of the reproductions of Staffordshire dogs.

Plate 6-22 offers a porcelain collection. Left to right: Rose Medallion bowl, cake stand, footed tray with dove, platter tray, footed bowl.

Now we come to something quite removed from realism, creations that are symbolic rather than realistic, a poetically spiritual approach to clay.

Here are two miniature scenes executed in an entirely different manner by the Korean artist Dong Hee Suh. Both of these handsome pieces are made of stoneware clay and have a salt glaze:

Plate 6-23: "The Holy City." This is a unique form of coil building with notched slabs and rhythmic flowing folds of coils—a thoroughly original approach to design. This piece measures 17″ x 5″. Photo by the artist.

Plate 6-24: "Glory." It is 7″ x 13½″. Photo by the artist.

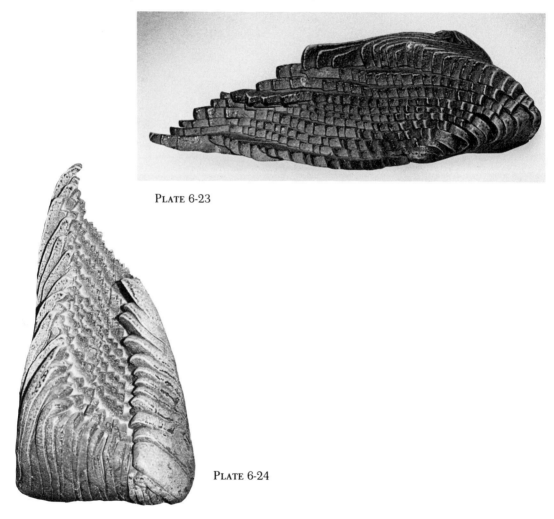

PLATE 6-23

PLATE 6-24

MOLDS

PLASTER OF PARIS is a big help to ceramists because of its ability to absorb moisture from clay. A spoonful of liquid clay (slip) dropped on a dry plaster slab will turn into a leather-hard button in just a minute or two. In an hour it will be dry enough to be put into a kiln and fired.

This property of plaster makes it possible to cast, or press, delicate shapes. Without plaster the beautiful extremely delicate porcelain figurines made during the fifteenth and sixteenth centuries would have been virtually impossible.

Plaster bats or smooth plaster slabs make good working surfaces; plaster bats are sometimes used in work on the potter's wheel.

Plaster of paris is gypsum rock (alabaster) that has been calcined (heated to a high temperature) to drive off its chemically combined water, then pulverized (ground to a fine powder). When mixed with water the powder sets into a hard mass, somewhat like the original rock.

U.S. Gypsum Company makes a special plaster for ceramic work. It comes in 100-lb. bags, but small quantities can be bought from dealers in ceramic supply or hobby shops under various names such as "hobby plaster," "casting plaster," etc.

MIXING PLASTER

Warning! Working with plaster is a messy business. Before starting, think about the problems of cleaning up afterward—spread layers of newspaper on the surface of the worktable.

Plaster can be mixed in any type of container, but most convenient are plastic bowls. For mixing small quantities of plaster, disposable containers are handy. An empty cottage-cheese box, for example, or a cut-down milk carton is just right for small jobs; and instead of washing it afterward, one can throw it away.

The proper ratio of plaster to water is 2¾ lbs. of plaster to 1 qt. of water, but if you don't have a scale, you can mix by eye.

PHOTO SERIES 21: *Mixing and Pouring Plaster*

1. We are going to pour a plaster slab using a chinaware dish as a form. In the foreground is a portion of a wooden slat from a defunct venetian blind. Our mixing bowl is an empty cottage-cheese container. We put water into the container and start sprinkling plaster into the water using a plastic spoon. We continue sprinkling plaster until a small mound remains above the water.

The plaster must now be allowed to stand undisturbed for a few minutes (this is called the *slaking* period). When the mound of plaster above the surface of the water has disappeared, there may be about ⅛″ of clear water above the plaster. If there is more than that, it should be poured off carefully into another container (or a potted plant) but NOT—NO, NEVER—into the sink.

After the plaster has slaked, it should be stirred, preferably with a plastic spoon. The spoon should scrape the bottom of the container so that all of the plaster is thoroughly mixed. In a few minutes, as stirring continues, the plaster will start to thicken. At this point, the plaster is ready to pour.

2. Pouring the plaster. As plaster begins to fill the dish, bubbles will rise
to the surface. These should be elimi-
nated by lifting the dish and tapping
it on the table several times. This will
force bubbles to the top where they
can be broken by blowing on them.
The plaster will be poured in until it
fills the dish just about to over-
flowing.

3. The pouring has been completed;
the piece of wood is drawn across the
top of the dish as shown to make a
smooth surface. Now we wait for the
plaster to set.

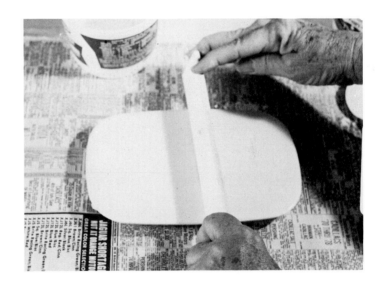

As the plaster sets it goes through the *cheese state*—it becomes about
as thick as cottage cheese, still soft but too thick to pour. After that the
plaster starts to crystallize and get hard. During the crystallization period
the plaster becomes warm, almost hot, to the touch. When crystallization
is complete the plaster starts to cool. After the plaster is thoroughly cold
(about forty-five minutes after pouring) it is safe to remove it.

4. The casting has set and cooled, it should now be easy to lift it out of the china dish. If you find it difficult to remove the casting, pouring cold water on it will help to loosen it. Should it still be reluctant to come out, a thin knife blade inserted at one end will make it pop right out.

SIZING

Plaster poured onto glass or a smooth porcelain or plastic surface will come away without sticking. The same is true of moist clay. Other surfaces such as wood, metal, or hard plaster or fired objects must be sized with a soap solution or Vaseline, or a commercial parting compound, otherwise the plaster will stick fast to what it has been poured on. Commercial parting compound, which can be purchased from ceramic supply dealers or hobby shops, is best for miniature work.

CLEANING UP

Remember when working with plaster, NOT ONE BIT OF PLASTER MUST GET INTO THE SINK DRAIN. After every job, wipe tools and bowls with dampened paper towels or newspaper and dispose of the paper as ordinary refuse.

If plaster hardens on the inside of the plastic bowl, it can be chipped off onto a newspaper when the plastic bowl is squeezed.

Plaster of paris is a good fertilizer. If you prefer, instead of wiping the bowl clean, you can wash it with cold water (no soap) and pour the water onto your lawn or even on your potted plants.

If some plaster gets on portions of your clothing, let it harden, then brush it off. If brushing does not remove all of the plaster, soak the garment in cool water—again, NO SOAP; hand scrub the fabric by rubbing it against itself.

How much plaster to mix? After a little experience you will know just how much to mix for each job. A good plan is to mix a bit more than you think you will need. The excess can always be used to make more plaster slabs upon which to work.

PHOTO SERIES 22: *A One-Piece Press Mold for Buttons and Small Ornaments*

1. A rectangle of glass has been laid on top of several sheets of newspaper. A retaining wall of clay 1½″ high has been built enclosing a rectangular area. Eight decorative buttons have been modeled in clay as well as two plain convex buttons. These have been pressed *firmly* against the glass (they MUST be firmly anchored; otherwise, they will float away when the plaster is being poured). *Do not* allow the buttons and retaining wall to dry.

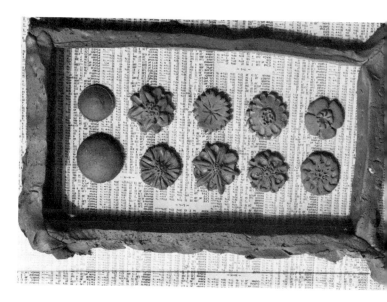

2. Plaster has been mixed in a plastic bowl. For better control during pouring, some of the plaster has been poured into the bottom half of a 1-qt. milk carton. This makes a good pouring shape. The plaster is poured around each form. Note the number of air bubbles appearing in the plaster. They must not be allowed to remain.

3. To get rid of the air bubbles, the sheet of glass is lifted at two corners and shaken vigorously.

4. The pouring is continued until the plaster reaches the top of the retaining wall. Any bubbles at that time will be removed by blowing gently on them. After the mold has set and cooled, the retaining wall may be removed. The clay used for the retaining wall will have scraps of plaster in it. This should be kept in a separate bag with a label on it saying "For mold work only."

5. The buttons are being removed from the mold. In the upper left a piece of moist clay pressed against the back of the button acts as a sort of handle that makes it easy to lift the clay out of the mold. At the right are depressions left in the mold after the clay buttons have been removed. Now the mold must dry (sunlight or warm oven).

6. Pressing a lump of clay into the mold to form a button.

7. Excess clay has been trimmed off the pressing.

8. Two button forms have been pressed and trimmed. At the lower right we see a round toothpick and a small strip of clay. This bit of clay will form a loop on the back of the button so that the button may be sewn to fabric.

9. Shaping the clay loop over the toothpick.

10. Attaching the loop to the back of the button.

11. Attaching the loop to the upper button.

12.   The buttons are lifted out of the mold. Again, a bit of moist clay helps to lift the button from the mold.

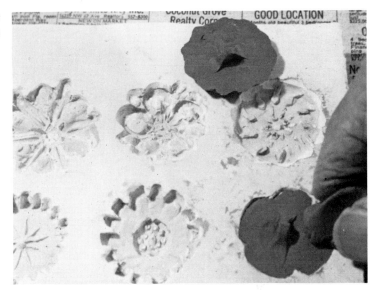

13.   A few buttons pressed from the mold. The two at top center are turned to show the fastening loops. Many of these were made by altering a pressing as soon as it came out of the mold and was still quite soft. For example, at the right end of the top row we see two circular buttons; immediately beneath them are two other buttons that were pressed into the same circular mold, then altered in shape.

PHOTO SERIES 23: *Another Press Mold*

1. We shall follow the steps used in making a press mold for buttons, except this time we model a simplified boy and girl and three birds.

2. The little clay figures are put into the dish that was used in Photo Series 21. Note that a ball of clay has been pressed against the side of the dish at the top and another one at the bottom. These will make finger grips so that the mold can be lifted from the dish easily after it has been set.

3. The mold has been poured. It has set, cooled, and dried. The original clay models have been removed. Pressings have been made in the three top depressions. Here clay is pressed into the depression at the lower right-hand corner of the mold.

4. Excess clay has been trimmed off with a potter's knife.

5. A piece of moist clay helps to lift the bird out of the mold.

6. Here are some pressings that have been glazed, fired, and decorated by methods described in chapter 13. They would make colorful Christmas tree ornaments.

chapter 8

SLIP AND SLIP CASTING

WE KNOW by now that liquid clay is called slip and that we can pour it into a mold to reproduce a form. Up to now, however, we have been using a prepared white low-fire casting slip we obtained from a dealer. For high-fire work, prepared casting slip can be purchased from a dealer also. But some ceramists prefer to prepare their own slip. This involves *deflocculation*.

Clay with enough water added to it so that it may be poured as a liquid is slip. But it takes too much water to make clay liquid. There is too much shrinkage as the slip dries, and complicated portions of a casting are apt to break off in the mold.

The plasticity of clay is believed to be due to an electrical or magnetic attraction that makes the tiny particles of clay flock together. Adding something to clay that destroys or reverses this electrical charge will make the particles repel one another instead of sticking together. With the addition of this substance a mass of clay that contains 35 percent water changes in consistency from a thick sticky mud to a free-flowing liquid. Substances that act on clay this way are called *electrolytes*. Sodium silicate and soda ash are the most frequently used electrolytes.

For most potters who make miniatures, buying commercially prepared casting slip that already contains deflocculating electrolytes is much simpler and usually less expensive than preparing their own. However, for those who do wish to prepare their own, instructions for deflocculation are given in the Appendix.

DRAIN MOLD FOR AN URN

All of the molds we have made so far have been press molds or solid-casting molds. Now let's try making a drain mold, one into which slip is poured and allowed to stand until a layer forms inside the mold. After that, all the slip that is still liquid is poured out—standard procedure for making bowl shapes.

PHOTO SERIES 24:   *Drain Molds for a Footed Urn*

1. We should have an electric potter's wheel for this project, but our mini-studio doesn't have room for one. What we are using here is a child's two-speed record player for which we have made a bat that fits over the turntable.

2. Here we are forming a solid lump of clay into the shape of an upside-down bowl with a flared rim. The turntable rotates slowly while the form is turned true. The depression at the top of the form is to receive the foot. At the upper left, resting on a sponge, is a piece of clay tentatively shaped into a foot for the urn.

3. Trying the foot for size. Our decision: the foot should be taller and wider at the base.

4. Preparing to pour the mold. A strip of medium-weight acetate serves as a retaining wall. A collar of clay has been pressed firmly all around the acetate strip. (Let's not have any leakage during pouring!) The exposed surface of the bat inside the retaining wall has been sized with two coats of parting compound. No sizing is needed on the acetate.

5. Pouring the plaster while the turntable slowly rotates.

6. The plaster has reached the cheese state; the retaining wall has been removed. A steel scraper is used to smooth the side of the mold.

7. The plaster has been allowed to set. After it went through the warm stage and then became thoroughly cold, the mold was lifted off the bat and the clay inside was removed.

8. The surface of the bat was scraped clean. The bat was removed for cleaning so that no particles of clay or plaster would get into the mechanism below the turntable. Next, a foot—taller and wider at the base than the original model—was shaped. A mold of the foot will be made by the same steps used in making the mold for the bowl.

9. Both molds were placed in a warm oven (120° F.) for two hours, by which time they were thoroughly dry. Here, slip has been poured into the molds.

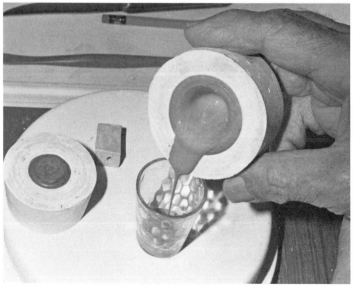

10. After fifteen minutes the slip that is still liquid is poured out of the larger mold.

11. The bowl mold stands upside down on two kiln props. The bowl for the foot will not be emptied. This means the foot will be heavier and stronger.

12. Once more, the bat has been scraped clean. A circle the same diameter as the top of the urn is being drawn on the bat as the wheel turns.

13. The bowl is centered upside down within the circle just drawn. A drop of slip is put into the depression that will hold the foot.

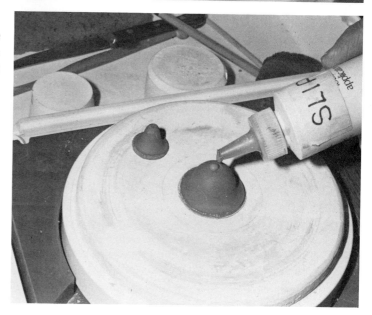

14.   Another drop of slip is placed on the foot.

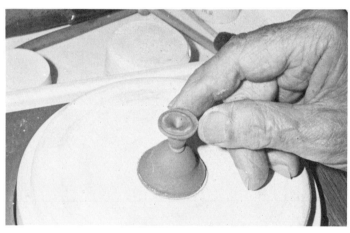

15.   The foot is attached to the bowl. The wheel is turned very slowly to check the positioning of the foot so that it will be perfectly centered and true.

16.   Three urns fired, glazed, and decorated with overglaze colors.

TWO-PIECE MOLDS

Two-piece molds are slightly more complicated. We could cover one-half of the model with a kind of shim made of clay, set up a retaining wall, then pour one-half of the mold. When the plaster has set we remove the clay shim, cut notches (to make the two parts of the mold fit together properly) in the half of the mold that has been poured, brush the surface of the first half of the mold with the parting compound, and then set up the retaining wall and pour the second half of the mold. The molds for the tail and the raised leg of the horse shown in Photo Series 28 were made this way.

Another method of making a two-piece mold of a very simple form is to slice it in half. Here are the steps:

PHOTO SERIES 25:   *Molds for Three Tiny Kings*

1.   Here is a pair of tiny figurines for a crèche, two of the three kings.

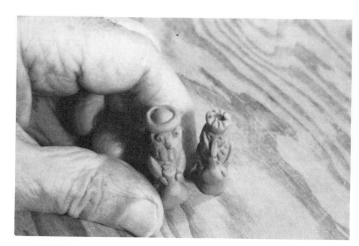

2.   One of the kings has been cut in two. One-half is placed face up on a small sheet of glass. The back half is shown at the left of the glass. The second king is being sliced in half.

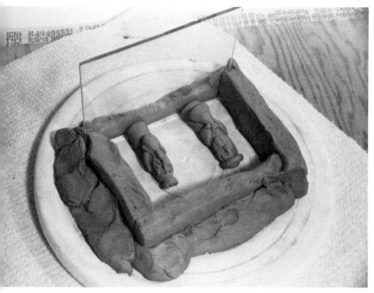

3. The front halves of the two kings are pressed firmly against a piece of glass. A second piece of glass is put in place as a retaining wall at their feet. Clay is used to build up the other three sides of the rectangular retaining wall.

4. Plaster has been mixed and poured to make the first half of the mold. The first half of the mold has the front halves of the two kings in place. The rear half of the king at the right has been put in position. The back half of the second king is about to be added.

5. Three notches are cut into the first half of the mold. A modeling tool with an oval end is pressed against the plaster and rotated to make these notches.

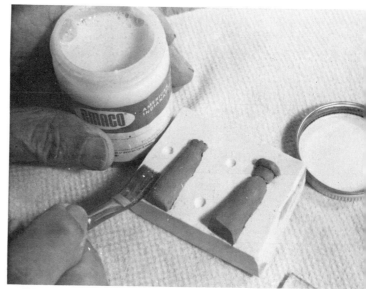

6. We must not forget sizing. The two back halves of the kings are in place. A coating of parting compound is brushed over the entire surface of the plaster. After it has dried, a second coat is brushed over it.

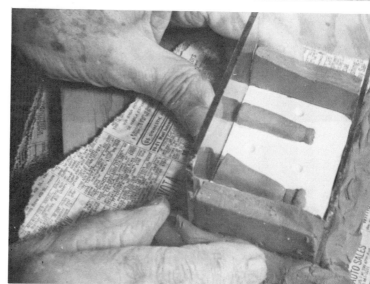

7. Retaining walls in place again. This time pieces of glass are used at the top and at the bottom while clay slabs form the sides.

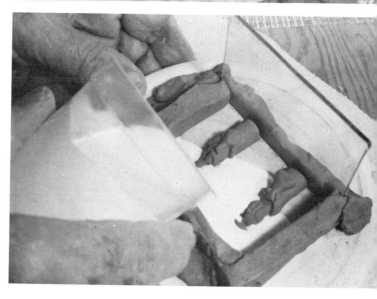

8. Pouring the second half of the mold.

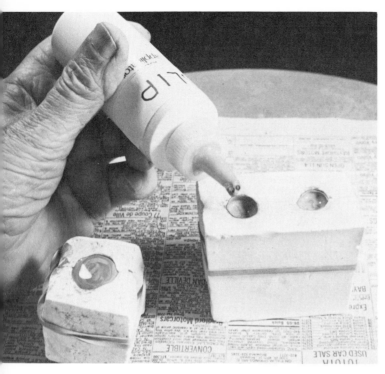

9. A two-piece mold for the third one of the three kings was made by a similar method. The two molds have dried; now the two halves of each mold are held together by rubber bands and slip is poured into the molds.

10. After fifteen minutes the excess slip was poured out of the molds, and the castings were allowed to become firm. At the left we see one of the kings removed from the mold. The second king is still halfway in the mold; the third king removed from his mold is shown at the right.

11. The finished pieces fired and glazed. The three kings also appear in the color section.

THREAD SEPARATION

Another method of making a two-piece mold is by thread separation. The model is pressed firmly onto a piece of glass, and the thread is put on the surface along the line where the two halves of the mold are to separate. The retaining wall is then set in place, and plaster is poured over the entire model. A moment after the plaster hardens into the cheese state, the thread, held at both ends, is pulled upward, thus dividing the mold into two parts. It is, of course, impossible to cut notches when using this method, but the slight irregularities made when the thread is pulled out make it possible to fit the two halves together perfectly. Here are the steps:

PHOTO SERIES 26:   *Crèche Figures—St. Joseph and Mary*

1.   Thread is being placed along the dividing line of the figurine of Mary. At the lower right is St. Joseph with the thread already in place. In the background we see two clay retaining walls that have been formed around a plastic pill bottle wrapped in newspaper.

2.   The thread is in place on each of the two figurines; the ends of the thread are being anchored to the glass with pellets of clay.

3. Retaining walls in place. The ends of the threads project beyond the retaining walls.

4. Plaster is spooned into one of the molds. Note that the plaster is not put into the mold until it has started to thicken slightly. Plaster poured too soon might wash the threads away from their positions on the figurines.

5. Plaster is spooned into the second mold.

6. Pulling up one of the threads. Timing is most important here. If pulled too soon, the two halves of the mold will reseal themselves. If we wait too long the plaster will harden, and we may find it impossible to pull the threads out. The thread must be pulled just as the plaster reaches the cheese state.

138

7. Pulling up the other thread.

8. The molds have set. The model of Mary has been removed from the mold at the left. Joseph is still in place in one half of the other mold.

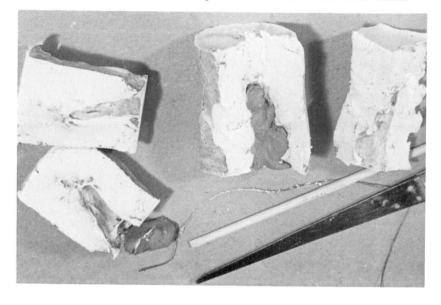

9. Finished crèche figures. Here we see a pair of castings that have been trimmed and another pair glazed with a white opaque Majolica glaze and fired.

10. The Holy Family. Overglaze colors were used to paint garments and features. The infant lies on a bed of straw that was made by pressing clay through a garlic press. The kneeling figure of Joseph is 1½″ high; that of Mary is 1⅛″ high.

PHOTO SERIES 27: *Pouring Slip into a Press Mold*

We had modeled a cluster of buildings to create an exotic street scene and had poured plaster over the model to make a press mold, but after making several pressings, we decided to try pouring slip instead of pressing clay.

Can a one-piece press mold be converted into a two-piece drain mold with the help of a slab of plaster? Let's try it.

1. Here we see the press mold and,
to its right, a smooth slab of plaster
that was cast against a piece of glass.

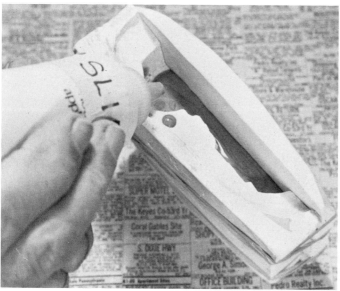

2. The plaster slab has been fastened to the press mold with rubber
bands. Slip is being poured in.

3. After the slip was firm enough
the slab was taken away, revealing
the casting of the street scene.

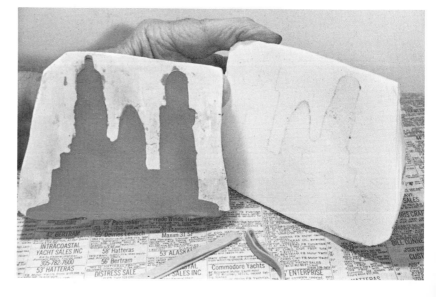

4. The casting as it came from the mold is shown at the left. At the right is a finished casting that has been trimmed, altered a bit (note the roof on the low building to the left), then glazed with white opaque glaze and fired to cone 06. After that it was decorated with overglaze colors and fired to cone 017.

A MULTIPLE-PIECE MOLD

The porcelain figurines that we see advertised in the fashionable magazines are remarkably complicated constructions, adorned with realistic detail. These creations are, of course, made in molds and the making of such molds requires the work of a team of artists and craftsmen working many hours a day for many days. First a sculptor models an animal or a bird or foliage in clay; then a *waste mold* is made, usually in two or more pieces. There is no worry about undercuts. When the waste mold is hard, the clay model is dug out and plaster of paris is poured in (after the inside of the waste mold has been sized, of course). After the plaster has set the waste mold is broken, and the plaster casting is then worked on by a sculptor who strives for absolute accuracy in detail—fur, feathers, etc. Then casting molds are made of various parts of the figurine. These separate parts are joined together to complete the assembled figurine.

Quite a difference from the work we saw Frank Eliscu doing, isn't it? The freedom and spontaneity are missing, but of course Eliscu was making one-of-a-kind figures, and was not engaged in mass production.

People who make miniatures for sale have told us that a knowledge of mold-making, even though the process may be complicated, is important. Let's make a mold of a little horse.

PHOTO SERIES 28:   *Making a Multiple-Piece Mold*

1.   A figure of a tiny horse has been modeled in clay. The space underneath the horse's belly has been filled in with clay. The horse stands on a turntable. In front of him are three tools that will play an important part in making the mold.

2.   The turntable has been given a half turn so we can see the other side. It is obvious that a mold including the tail and the raised leg would be extremely complicated to make. We shall detach these and make separate molds of them.

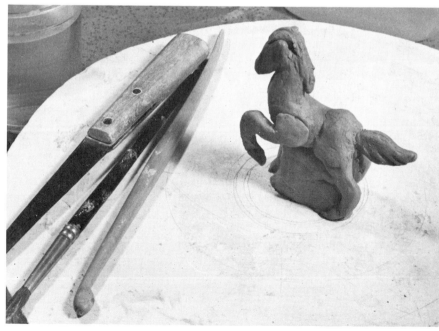

3. The tail and the raised leg have been removed. At the lower right we see the leg embedded halfway in a slab of soft clay. Notches have been made with the round end of the modeling tool. A bit of clay has been added at the top of the leg to provide a pouring vent. At the left we see the tail embedded halfway in a slab of clay and a notch being made. The two strips of clay (quite plastic) will serve as retaining walls for each of the molds.

4. The retaining walls are in place around the tail and the leg. Walls of clay (the clay should be plastic) have been pressed against the front and the back of the figure. Two more clay walls have been fastened against the first two, leaving space on either side of the horse for the plaster to be poured. The work must now be lifted off the turntable so that a piece of glass may be placed underneath it.

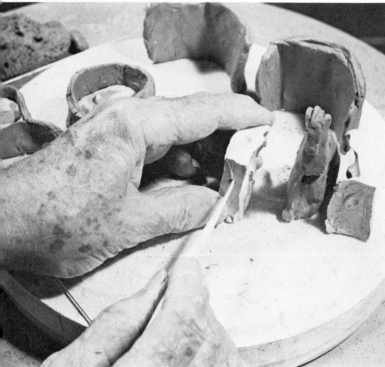

5.   Glass is on the turntable. The two side pieces have been poured and so has the tail. Plaster is now poured into the leg mold.

6.   The first four pourings have set and cooled. Notches must now be cut in the ends of the two side pieces. After this the ends of the side pieces must be sized—given at least two coats of parting compound. Note that we must take care not to get any size on the inner portions of the mold because that would make the plaster nonabsorbent and our mold would not work. (If any size does get on an inner surface, that surface will have to be carefully scraped clean before the mold is used.)

   In the upper left are the molds of the tail and the leg. Their plaster surfaces have been sized. In the upper right are two clay slabs that will serve as retaining walls for the lower part of the figure mold.

7. Putting retaining walls in place for the front end and the back end of the lower portion of the mold. These retaining walls must be pressed *firmly* against the two completed portions of the mold that enclose the body of the horse to prevent a retaining wall from giving way while the plaster is being poured.

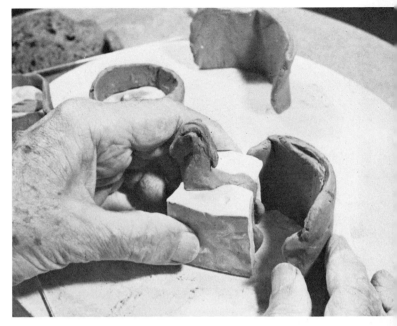

8. The four pieces of the lower portion of the mold have been poured and allowed to set. Notches have been cut in the upper surfaces of these four bottom pieces and the surfaces have been sized. Here a clay slab is set in position to form a retaining wall for one-half of the top portion of the mold. At the upper center we see the molds of the leg and the tail.

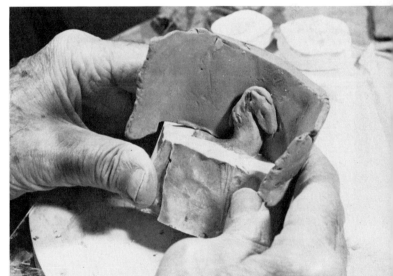

9. The retaining wall for the second half of the top portion is being put in place.

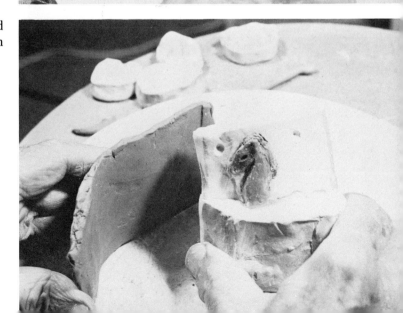

10. Pouring casting slip into the mold. All the parts are held firmly together by rubber bands. Slip is poured only into one of the three leg openings; when the slip rises to the tops of the other two leg openings, we know that the mold has been completely filled.

11. As water is absorbed from the slip, the level of slip in each leg will sink. More slip must be added to fill each opening. To make a casting that is sufficiently strong we must continue adding slip until the level stops falling.

The mold must *not* be opened until the slip has had time to become firm. This may take several hours. If the outside of the mold feels cool and damp to the touch, it is too soon to open. The setting time may be shortened by putting the mold into a *warm* oven (120° F.) with the door propped open for an hour or two.

12. Disassembling the mold.

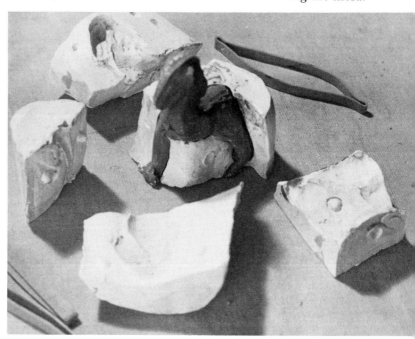

13. The underbelly piece of the mold is still in place. The tail has been attached. Now the front leg is being put in place. Slurry is brushed on the portions to be joined.

14. All parts of the horse are in place. The underbelly has not yet been removed. At this point seams can be trimmed off and changes in the modeling may be made if desired (we could even add a horn and curly tail tip to convert the horse into a unicorn).

15. The underbelly piece has been removed. Finishing touches with a brush dipped in slip.

16. Three castings from the mold. Two of them have been fired and glazed.

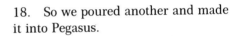

17. Changing the horse into a unicorn was such fun.

18. So we poured another and made it into Pegasus.

chapter · 9

CARVING MOLDS

THIS IS *intaglio*—cutting in, instead of building up. It's a kind of three-dimensional design in reverse in which one must think backwards. We became interested in this kind of designing when we started to make sand castings on the beach in front of our Florida home—so interested, in fact, that we wrote a book about it *(Creative Design in Sand Casting,* Crown Publishers, Inc.).

Earlier, in chapter 7, we discussed plaster of paris. Remember how we spoke about always having something handy such as a piece of glass or an empty plastic container, so that when we had mixed too much plaster for a mold, we could make either a slab or a form that would be useful?

Well, here in plate 9-1 we see how such a form can be used to make a press mold. At the upper left is an empty plastic container. Leaning against it is the shape that resulted when excess plaster had been poured into it. In the center of the picture is a similar shape into which a sun face has been carved. In the foreground are two pressings from the mold. The one on the left has been trimmed. At the right are the tools that were needed to make the carving.

One of these pressings, glazed and fired by the raku method, is shown in the top center of the jewelry plate in the color section.

PLATE 9-1

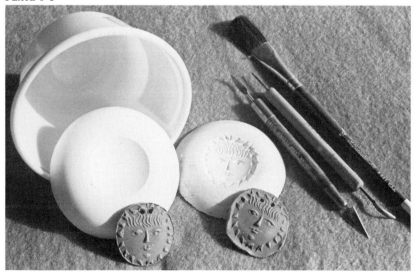

AN INCISED MOLD FOR A PICTURE FRAME

At the right in plate 9-2 we see a plaster slab. A mold for a miniature picture frame has been carved into this slab with the tools shown. On the plaster slab at the left are three pressings from the mold. The one at the upper right shows a pressing in which the clay is still plastic. To the left is a pressing in which the center portion has been cut out. At the bottom is a pressing that has become bone dry. We could, if we wished, use this bottom pressing to paint a picture on either with underglaze or overglaze colors within the frame area. The tiny frame is 2″ wide by 3″ tall.

One important tool missing from this picture is the dry soft-haired paintbrush. As you carve you must constantly brush the plaster dust out of the carving in order to see what you're doing.

The sun face shown in plate 9-1 was carved directly, without any drawing having been made first. For the picture frame, a pencil drawing was made on tracing paper. The paper was then reversed and taped to the plaster. The sketch was then traced onto the plaster by drawing along all the lines with a sharp pencil.

Plate 9-3 shows the pressing in which the center was cut out, glazed, and fired. Now it frames a reproduction of a painting by an old master that was cut from a page of a magazine.

In plate 9-4 more carving has been done into the picture frame mold—a woman's head in profile. The idea was suggested by an early

ich Pots. Alan Schnepel. 2½″–3″ tall, raku.

low top: Ceramic Table and *Chinaware* for doll's house. Evelyn
rid. Scale 1″ to 1′.

low bottom: Park with Fountain. Kenny. 7½″ wide, 8″ deep, pond
diameter. Children, 1½″; dog, 1″.

Herons. Frank Eliscu. 4″ tall.

Mold-made pieces, *Three Kings*, cast, 1½″ 1¾″. *Boy*, 2″; and *Girl*, 1¾″, pressed. Kenny.

Replica of the *Porseleinkamer*, which ca be seen full scale at the Rijksmuseum Amsterdam. Dee Snyder. 13″ x 11″ (scale to 1′).

Red Fox. Frank Eliscu. 3″ tall.

Daddy at Ease. Carla Kenny. 2½″ high.

Miniature Wheel-thrown Vases, porcelain with crystalline glazes. David Snair. 1¼″ to 4″ high. Photos by the artist.

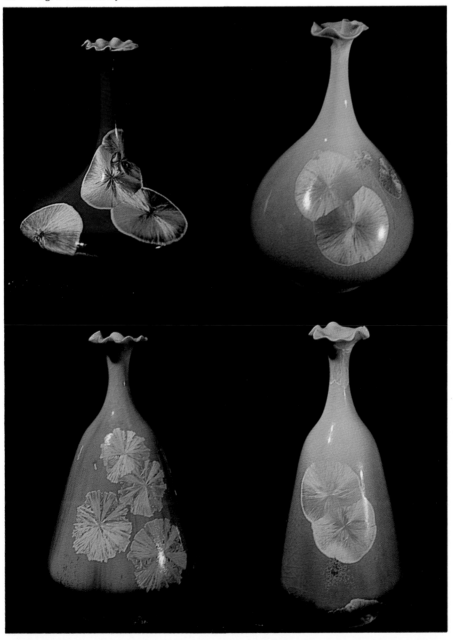

Wheel-thrown Mini Pots. Christ▶
Rogers. 1½″ to 1¾″ tall.

Renaissance Street Scenes.
Kenny. 4½″ high x 5″ wide, cast
from same mold.

Cat Pendant. Betsy Stoinoff. ▶
diameter. *Tired Teenager* (1½′
and *Stick Pin* (1″). Carla Kenny.

Christmas Tree Ornaments. Mexican. ½" to 2".

Whistles—*Two Mexican Ponies,* 3" high, and two *Porcelain "Critters,"* 1½" high. Vina Schemer.

Jalisco Ware. Mexican. Vase 1½" tall, pheasant and cat 1" x 2".

House and Garden. Kenny. Bowl (a pinch pot) 5¼" x 3¾" x 1" high. House (slab built) 3" x 1¾" x 3¾" tall. House has stained-glass windows.

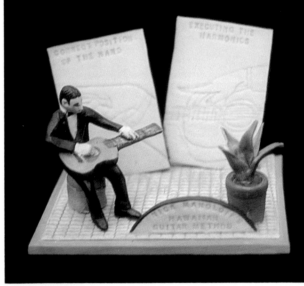

Nick Manoloff's Hawaiian Guitar Method. Chris Unterseher. Base 3½" x 3½". Photo by Ted Cook.

Jordenaires with Patsy Cline and Jerry Byrd on Steel Guitar. Chris Unterseher. Base 6" x 4". Photo by Ted Cook.

Toothpick People and *Recipe Card Holders.* Lee and Dorothy Shank. The former wheel-thrown, the latter hand-modeled, 1½″ to 1¾″.

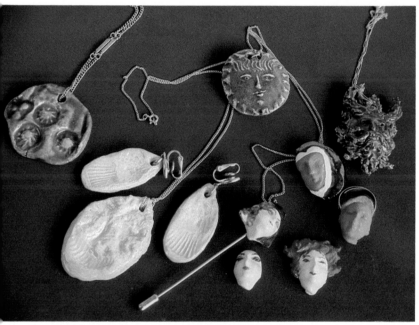

Glaze samples—*Lion's Head,* hand built; *Sun Faces,* pressed in mold. Kenny. 1″ to 1½″ diameter.

Candleholder and *Mirror Frame.* Irene Batt. Raku, each 2″ high.

Mermaid Fountain. Kenny. Mermaid 5″ tall, overall height 7½″.

New York Brownstone. Carla Kenny. Garden, 10″ x 6″ x 2¾″, house 8½″ tall, both earthenware.

Crèche. Mexican. 2½″ high x 3½ x 3″.

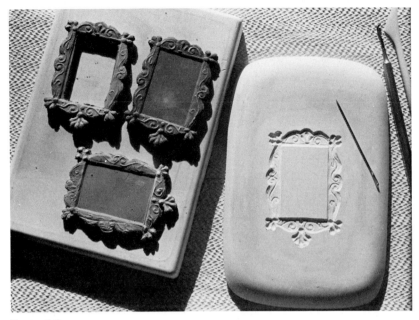

PLATE 9-2

PLATE 9-3

PLATE 9-4

PLATE 9-5

PLATE 9-6

eighteenth-century porcelain plaque. In the lower portion at the right we see a pressing that has been glazed, fired, and decorated with overglaze pigments. After the firing, the frame was covered with gold leaf, not real gold leaf, but the less expensive pseudogold leaf purchased in a hobby shop.

A CARVED DRAPE MOLD

Plate 9-5 shows the making of a drape mold. This type of mold (we used to call them "flop-over" molds) is one in which a layer of clay is formed by being draped over a plaster mound. To make this mold, a bit of excess plaster that had been poured into a small plastic container was carved. The whole surface was cut down, leaving a mound in the center into which the outline of a fish was incised. Tiny layers of clay were rolled and pressed over the hump. While the clay layer was on the hump, it was trimmed and a tiny coil of clay was used to make a foot. The pressing must be left on the hump until it is firm. The two pressings are shown with the raised design. One of them has been trimmed a little more closely than the other. At the left is a finished glazed and fired platter. This measures 1⅝″ long, which is equivalent to a 20″-serving platter full size.

At the bottom is a trimming tool and a round-ended file for smoothing the rim.

In plate 9-6 we see a pair of angels that were pressed in a mold carved out of a slab of plaster that was cast in the bottom of a large cottage-cheese container. These winged ladies are 3¼″ tall.

chapter 10

CLAY

FOR MINIATURE work we do not need to learn too much chemistry, but we should have some basic knowledge about what clay is and how it came to be, and we should also be familiar with some of the minerals most important to potters.

Our earth contains over a hundred known elements (105 last time we counted), but only a few of these are of interest to the potter. Silicon (Si) and aluminum (Al) when combined with oxygen (O) become silica (SiO_2) and alumina (Al_2O_3). Pure clay is one part alumina and two parts silica plus chemically combined water ($Al_2O_3 \cdot 2SiO_2 \cdot 2H_2O$).

Note that chemically combined water has nothing to do with plasticity.

FELDSPAR

There was no clay in the beginning when the ball of fire that was to become the globe we live on cooled and formed a rocky crust. Clay is a product of change. Feldspar, the chief ingredient of granite rock, is composed of alumina, silica, and alkaline substances (potash, soda, and others). These alkaline substances are soluble in water. As rocks are weathered for many many years by glaciers and winds and rain, these alkaline substances are washed out—what remains is clay.

But enough of chemistry. Here's a brief review of clays and clay bodies.

RESIDUAL CLAY

This is clay that has remained where it was formed. There is no such thing as *pure* clay, but this is the closest thing to it. Kaolin (or china clay) is coarse-grained, not very plastic, and highly refractory (resistant to heat)—almost pure white both before and after firing. It's too refractory to fire in a ceramic kiln, so fluxes must be added.

SEDIMENTARY CLAYS

These have been carried great distances from their points of origin by winds and streams and ice. They are more plastic than residual clay because they have been ground finer. In the course of their travels they have picked up impurities, hence they are more plastic and fire at lower temperatures and to different colors. There is almost an infinite variety of sedimentary clays:

Plastic kaolin (EPK). Is more workable than regular kaolin and fires white.

Ball clay. This is a clay carried by streams and deposited under water. It has a fine grain, contains carbonaceous material, and is highly plastic. When dug it is dark in color, but it fires almost pure white. It is an important ingredient in porcelain bodies.

Stoneware clay. This is a plastic clay that matures in the range between cones 5 and 10. It usually fires light buff. In reduction firing it produces beautiful shades of dark brown.

Common clay. Here is the clay that is used for making low-fired earthenware. It contains iron and other impurities that lower its firing range. It matures between cone 08 and cone 03.

Bentonite. This is a clay formed by volcanic action that contains colloidal matter. It is extremely plastic. Bentonite is never used to form objects, but a small percentage of it added to a clay body greatly improves its working properties. It must be mixed with the other body ingredients in powder form.

Fire clay. A rough-textured, highly refractory clay that is not very plastic. It is used in stoneware bodies.

Grog is clay that has been fired and then ground up and screened. When it is added to clay it provides openings through which moisture can escape so that thick pieces will not crack during firing. For most work 30/

60-mesh grog is used—that is, grog fine enough to go through a screen with 30 meshes to the inch but too coarse to go through one with 60 meshes to the inch.

Terra cotta. This is a common clay of coarse grain that dries with a minimum of warping. It is used in clay sculpture and in the manufacture of building tiles. This clay is also used for garden pottery and storage jars.

Talc (soapstone). A valuable ingredient in whiteware bodies, it has a wide firing range, cone 05 to cone 8. Talc is remarkable for its low shrinkage during firing.

Potters who make big pieces get a kick out of making their own clay bodies according to formulas they work out themselves. Some enjoy the thrill of digging their own clay. All of that takes time and also requires a lot of studio space, for storage of materials, machines for mixing, bats for drying, and so on.

Our advice to miniaturists: decide what kind of work you want to do (low-fire? high-fire?) and how you plan to do it (throwing? casting? hand forming?), then get a ceramic supply dealer's catalog or talk to your local hobby supplier and buy a ready-made body just right for your needs.

GLAZES

THE GLASS coating that melts onto clay during the fire gives beauty and color; it seals the pores of low-fire ware to make it waterproof; it makes tiles and outdoor sculpture able to withstand the ravages of wind and weather.

Every glaze must have three main ingredients: a glass-forming substance (silica); alumina to give the glaze body and keep it from running off the ware; and a flux, or fluxes, to make all the ingredients fuse together.

Fluxes work at different temperatures: for low-fire ware, lead and the alkaline minerals (potash, soda, lime) are good fluxes; for stoneware, feldspar and zinc are used; for porcelain, feldspar alone is sufficient.

Ingredients are added to glazes for special effects. Oxides of tin and zirconium, for example, make a transparent glaze semiopaque or opaque. Note that tin right now is in short supply and very expensive, so it's smart to rely on zirconium, which potters use in oxide forms called zircopax or ultrox.

Glazes are classified according to the flux they contain, according to their temperature, whether they are for high fire or low fire, or whether they contain the alkaline substances (potash, soda)—thus we would speak of a high-fire feldspathic glaze, etc.

CLASSIFICATION OF GLAZES

Lead. Before we go any further, heed this warning: LEAD IS A POISON. Raw oxides of lead (red lead, white lead, litharge) MUST NEVER be admitted to the miniaturist's studio.

But we *can* use lead with impunity if it is in a frit. Frits are glazes that have been fired, then pulverized.

Frit 3304, made by the Ferro Enamel Company, is a good all-purpose high-lead frit for glazes that fire from cone 08 to cone 02.

Ferro frit 3134 is a leadless borosilicate. These and many other frits can be bought from dealers.

There are many advantages to using frits. Besides making lead less toxic, fritting makes the ingredients in alkaline glazes insoluble. Raw materials used in glazes contain substances that burn out during the firing and go up the chimney as waste. Frits don't have any such waste substances.

Alkaline glazes. These are leadless glazes that use soda, borax, potash, or other alkalis as fluxes.

Color in glazes. The table in figure 11-1 lists a number of things that can be added to glazes to provide color. The last column in this table describes colors produced in a reduction fire. Reduction is described in chapter 12.

Slip glazes. A clay that matures at cone 04 will melt into a liquid at cone 6, so a slip made of that clay applied to a stoneware pot and fired to cone 6 or higher becomes a glaze (one of Chris Clark's castles was glazed this way).

Egyptian paste. This is a mixture of clay and soda with oxides added. Small objects modeled out of this material and fired to cone 07 come out of the fire glazed. Dealers sell this in dry powder form in a variety of colors, but the only true Egyptian paste is a beautiful turquoise blue. Some bits of jewelry made of yellow Egyptian paste are shown in the color section.

Crystalline glazes. David Snair's four porcelain vases shown in the color section are fine examples of what happens when zinc silicate crystals form during the cooling of a molten glaze. Getting such crystals to form is a complicated, time-consuming, and costly technique that is recommended only for the most experienced potter.

We have not included any of David's glaze recipes in the section that follows because it would take several pages to explain how to put his recipes to use. David has done a lot of research and made hundreds of tests before achieving the results shown in his color photographs. We hope that someday he will write a book about it.

Our survey of glaze materials has been brief (we didn't say a word about the many kinds of feldspar or mention the other minerals that are close relations of feldspar, such as nepheline syenite), but in the glossary you will find a more complete listing, together with definitions of ceramic terms.

Figure 11-1. COLORING ADDITIONS FOR GLAZES

Oxide	Percent	Color in Lead Glaze	Color in Alkaline Glaze	Color When Reduced
Chromium oxide	2%	Vermilion at cone 012 Brown at cone 06 Green at cone 02		
Cobalt carbonate	0.5%	Medium blue	Medium blue	Medium blue
	1%	Strong blue	Strong blue	Strong blue
Copper carbonate	0.5%			Copper red
	1%	Green	Turquoise	Deep red
	2–3%	Deep green	Turquoise	Red and black
	8%	Green with metallic areas	Blue green with metallic areas	
Ilmenite	3%	Tan specks	Gray black specks	Spotty brown
Iron chromate	2%	Gray brown	Gray	
Iron oxide	1%			Celadon
	2%	Pale amber	Pale tan	Olive green celadon
	4%	Red brown	Brown	Mottled green
	10%	Dark red	Black brown	Saturated iron red
Manganese carbonate	4%	Purple brown	Purple violet	Brown
Nickel oxide	2%	Gray brown	Gray	Gray blue
Rutile	5%	Tan	Gray brown	
Vanadium stain	6%	Yellow	Yellow	
Cobalt carbonate Iron oxide	0.5% 2%	Gray blue	Gray blue	
Cobalt carbonate Manganese carbonate	0.5% 4%	Blue purple	Aubergine	
Cobalt carbonate Rutile	0.5% 3%	Gray blue	Gray blue	Textured blue
Copper carbonate Rutile	3% 3%	Textured green	Textured blue green	
Ilmenite Rutile	2% 2%	Textured brown	Textured gray brown	Spotty brown
Iron oxide Cobalt carbonate Manganese carbonate	8% 1% 3%			Black
Cobalt carbonate Iron oxide Manganese carbonate	3% 2% 2%	Mirror black		
Manganese carbonate Iron oxide	6% 3%	Luster brown		

Salt glaze. This is a special type of glaze that is made by throwing salt into the firing chamber of a kiln when the temperature reaches cone 8. The kiln must be one which burns fuel (not an electric one). The salt volatilizes and sits upon the ware, forming a hard glaze with a kind of orange-peel texture. Since the salt vapor settles on the inside of the kiln as well as the ware, a salt-glaze kiln CANNOT be used for any other type of work. The pieces in plate 6-23, "The Holy City," and plate 6-24, "Glory" by Dong Hee Suh, have a salt glaze.

GLAZING

Glazes can be applied to ware by spraying, but this requires a booth and a spray gun. Miniature pieces can be dipped, but for real tiny pieces it's best to use a brush. Plate 11-1 shows a little cup held on the handle of a crochet hook while glaze is painted on. Note the egg carton in which commercial glazes have been mixed with water. Each cup has been identified with a waterproof felt-tip pen.

Plate 11-2 shows the glazing of Joseph and Mary: they were held by the feet, then placed on newspaper for the last touches. Note at the upper left a plastic tray that once held frozen hors d'oeuvres. This makes a carrying tray for the trip to the kiln.

PLATE 11-1

PLATE 11-2

Gums enable glaze to be applied more easily to pottery. Gum acts as a binder to hold the glaze on the ware so that there is less danger of glaze being rubbed off when the ware is handled. When one glaze is put over another it is advisable to brush gum over the first glaze before applying the second. Gum also helps in overglaze painting. Several types of gum can be used with glazes—among them, gum tragacanth, CMC, and others; but we have found that for miniature work, buying prepared gum solution makes more sense than preparing your own.

SOME GLAZE RECIPES
Quantities Given in Percentages

Low-fire
- Transparent fritted glaze. Cone 07 to 04.
    - Frit 3304 90
    - Ball clay 10
  To make opaque white add 10 percent Zircopax.

- Alkaline Majolica fritted glaze. Cone 07 to cone 04.
    - Frit 3134 90
    - Ball clay 10
  To make opaque white add 10 percent Zircopax.

- Colemanite or borosilicate glaze. Cone 06 to cone 04.

    Colemanite 30
    Feldspar 45
    Zinc oxide 5
    Barium carbonate 6
    China clay 4
    Flint 10

Middle range

- Stoneware glaze. Cone 5 to cone 9.

    Feldspar 35
    Dolomite 16
    Whiting 6
    China clay 9
    Flint 34

High-fire

- Porcelain glaze. Cone 12 to cone 15.

    Feldspar 27
    Whiting 20
    China clay 20
    Flint 33

All of our work shown in this book was made in the low-fired range (our kiln goes only as high as cone 02), and practically all of our materials were commercially prepared. We had two full 4-oz. jars of glaze, one clear, one opaque; our sample glaze collections in powder form packaged in small envelopes (just had to add water); two palette pans of semimoist underglaze colors, and a half-dozen tiny jars of liquid glazes—all fitting into two shoe boxes. With all of these we were able to glaze a surprisingly large number of pieces.

Once again, our advice to the miniaturist: buy ready-made.

chapter 12

FIRE

SINCE THE DISCOVERY thousands of years ago that fire makes clay hard and vitreous, potters have been stoking their kilns with many different kinds of fuels, among them wood, coal, sometimes dried dung, and more recently oil and old rubber tires. Two newcomers among the sources of heat are gas and electricity.

For those who work entirely in miniature ceramics, an electric kiln is the best bet; it makes firing quicker and easier, and it takes up much less room.

Amaco makes a large number of kilns. Plate 12-1 shows their #HF-66 kiln that has an 11″ x 11″ x 11″ chamber, uses a 110–120-volt circuit, and fires to cone 8. This kiln can be supplied with a built-in pyrometer.

Plate 12-2 shows an octagon Duncan kiln with a 17¾″ x 20″ chamber. It is furnished with an automatic kiln sitter, requires a 240-volt circuit, fires to porcelain temperatures.

The Nova is a new concept in kiln design planned specifically for ceramists who work at home. It uses ceramic-fiber insulation instead of traditional firebrick, hence it is comparatively light in weight; it can be easily moved and stored. The Nova Senior, shown in plate 12-3, has a chamber 8″ in diameter at the bottom, 4″ in diameter at the top, with a total height of 12″; it fires to cone 6.

The Nova China Painter's Kiln (plate 12-4) has a chamber 12¼″ in diameter, 6½″ high. It fires to cone 04 and weighs 35 pounds.

The Seeley Doll Kiln shown in plate 12-5 is specially designed for miniature work. Its chamber measures 6½″ x 6½″ x 4½″. It uses 120-volt current, can be plugged into a house circuit, and fires to cone 8. For larger pieces a 2″-blank ring can be purchased that increases the height of the firing chamber.

PLATE 12-1

PLATE 12-2

PLATE 12-3

PLATE 12-4

We use a SNO C-4-S Kiln that stands on a concrete block in a corner of our living room when it is too windy to fire it on our terrace (plate 12-6). Our kiln uses 120-volt current, but it can be fired only to cone 02. The SNO Mini-Kiln (plate 12-6A) is excellent for miniature work up to 6″ wide and 4″ deep. It uses a 120-volt current and fires to cone 8. Its chamber is 6½″ x 6½″ x 4½″. The SNO Kiln shown in plate 12-7 uses a 240-volt current, fires to cone 8. Its chamber measures 14⅜″ x 14⅜″ x 13½″.

Professional miniaturists who make accessories for dollhouses would be wise when buying a kiln to invest in one that will fire to cone 8 or a bit higher.

PLATE 12-5

PLATE 12-6

PLATE 12-6a

PLATE 12-7

STACKING A KILN

Stacking greenware is no problem, but glazed pieces will stick fast to anything that touches the glazed surfaces during the fire.

A piece with glaze on the bottom must be fired standing on a stilt In miniature work it is best not to rely upon stilts, but to keep bottoms free of glaze.

The best way to fire a small figurine that is glazed is to scrape the bottom portion as clean as possible. Press a tiny pellet of clay into a pancake and let it dry, then brush it with kiln wash and stand the figurine on the kiln-washed disc. If the figurine and the clay pancake should stick together, it would not be difficult to chip them apart.

Kiln wash. To protect kiln shelves from bits of glaze that might fall onto them, paint them with a coating or two of kiln wash made of equal parts of flint and china clay mixed with water until the mixture is the consistency of cream. Kiln wash does not fuse during the firing, so any glaze that falls on it may be easily chipped off.

Kiln wash should be brushed on the floor of the kiln and on the top surface of the kiln shelves, never on the underside of a shelf. (Kiln wash on the underside of a shelf could flake off and fall onto glazed pieces.)

Miniaturists who don't have room to store materials like china clay and flint can buy dry kiln wash in small quantities from ceramic supply dealers.

Firing jewelry. Beads and pendants can be hung on a nichrome wire that rests on props (plate 12-8).

KILN TEMPERATURES

Pyrometric cones. A cone is a long thin triangular pyramid of clay with fluxes added so that it will melt at a known temperature. A number indicating its temperature is stamped into the side of the cone. When the potter fires his kiln he puts a series of cones into a lump of clay called a cone pat. This is put into the kiln in a position where it can be seen through the peephole. The series of cones should include three cones, one of the temperature to which the kiln is to be fired, one lower, and one

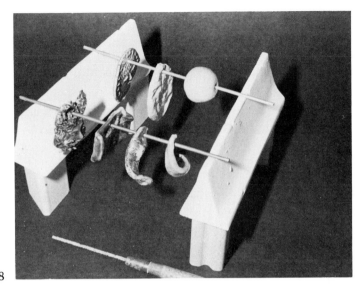

PLATE 12-8

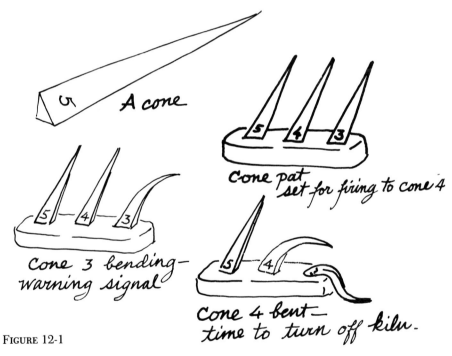

5 A cone

Cone pat set for firing to cone 4

Cone 3 bending—
warning signal

Cone 4 bent—
time to turn off kiln.

FIGURE 12-1

higher. Thus, if the potter is firing ware that matures at cone 07 (1814°F.), he should use cones 06, 07, 08. Cone 08, as we see by the cone table (see Appendix), bends at 1742°F., 07 bends at 1814°F., and 06 bends at 1859°F. The cones are set at a slant as shown in figure 12-1, tipping toward cone 08—the one that will bend first. The clay out of which the cone pat is made should contain grog to prevent it from cracking during the firing, but if no grog is available, holes punched into the cone pat with the point of a pencil or an orangewood stick will serve the same purpose.

As the temperature of the kiln rises and reaches 1700°F., cone 08 will start to bend. This is a warning signal to the potter; he continues the firing until cone 07 bends and then shuts off the kiln before cone 06 has started to bend. This shows that the kiln has reached 1814°F. without going far beyond it.

Cones come in two sizes: 1⅛″ and 2½″. The miniaturist, of course, uses the smaller cones.

Pyrometers. An electric pyrometer is another way of measuring kiln temperatures. It uses a metal bead that is made by soldering two different elements together—usually platinum and rhodium. When such a bead is heated, a tiny electric current is generated by a thermocouple, and an ammeter attached to the bead measures the current and translates it into degrees of temperature. Pyrometers of this type are available for use with any electric kiln. As a rule the company from which you buy your kiln will provide a pyrometer to go with it if you wish.

KILN SITTERS

Some kilns come with kiln sitters. These are safety devices that automatically turn off the current when the kiln reaches the desired temperature or when it has fired for a specific length of time.

THE FIRING SCHEDULE

For firing large pieces the advice has always been, go slowly. Not so for miniature work. A friend of ours, who uses a small electric test kiln with 6″ x 6″ x 6″ chamber, fires his pieces to cone 05 in less than an hour and a half and opens his kiln an hour and a half after he has turned it off.

Our kiln requires three hours to reach cone 06. We don't need a pyrometer or a kiln sitter; we use an alarm clock. When we close our kiln and turn it on, we set our alarm to remind us when two and a half hours have elapsed. From then on we look through the peephole every ten minutes, and sure enough, when the three hours are up, it is time to turn the kiln off.

A WORD ABOUT FIRE—
OXIDATION AND REDUCTION

Combustion is the union of carbon with oxygen. Fuels that burn are organic matter—combinations of carbon, oxygen, hydrogen, and nitrogen. If there is a plentiful supply of oxygen, the fire burns with a clear blue flame and we have an *oxidizing* atmosphere in which carbon dioxide (CO_2), water vapor, and nitrogen go up the chimney. If the oxygen supply is not sufficient or if too much carbon is in the kiln, the fire will smoke, producing carbon monoxide (CO) plus free carbon (soot). Carbon has a great affinity for oxygen and given a chance will steal it from other substances including clay and glazes. When that happens, we have a *reducing* atmosphere.

Interesting things happen to clay and glazes during reduction. Buff-clay bodies become darker, sometimes black. Green oxide of copper in a glaze loses some of its oxygen and becomes a red copper oxide, producing the beautiful *sang-de-boeuf* or oxblood glaze. Red oxide of iron loses some of its oxygen and becomes black oxide of iron, which gives us the soft gray green of celadon.

Reduction firing is often used for high-fire work with porcelain or stoneware. At low temperatures reduction is something the potter usually tries to avoid.

RAKU

The method of making ceremonial teabowls originated in Japan a few hundred years ago. Small hand-fashioned bowls (pinch pots) were bisque fired, then glazed. When the glazes dried, the bowls were thrust into red-hot kilns just long enough for the glazes to melt, then they were removed with tongs and put into pails with straw, leaves, or other organic matter. More organic matter was piled on top and the pails were covered. After a few minutes in this reducing atmosphere the bowls were taken out with tongs and thrust into cold water.

American potters have become enthusiastic about raku. They do not limit themselves to pinch pots but often make large pieces.

It is a simple matter for contemporary potters working in miniature to achieve reduction by using the raku process: small pieces are glazed and put into an electric kiln; when they become red-hot they are taken out with tongs and thrust into a can containing dry organic material, then covered tightly. This puts them in a reducing atmosphere. After a few minutes of reduction they are taken out and plunged into a bucket of cold water. Plate 12-9 shows Irene Batt placing the candle holder (red-hot) that she made in Photo Series 6 into her raku can that she keeps filled with dried vegetation.

She immediately covered the can, then took the red-hot mirror frame that she made in Photo Series 5 out of the kiln and put it into the smouldering raku can as shown in plate 12-10. (Note: the two pieces must not touch each other.) The cover was put on the can tightly again, and after a few minutes of reduction both of the miniature objects were lifted out with tongs and plunged into cold water. Irene then hosed down the contents of the raku can to put out the smouldering fire.

The sun-face pendant (top center in the jewelry plate in the color section) was fired by the raku method. Our raku pail is an empty coffee can with an old heavy cast-aluminum pot lid that fits snugly on the can.

PLATE 12-9

PLATE 12-10

TWO TEMPERATURES IN ONE FIRE

When we fire our kiln we frequently put ware glazed with 06 glazes on the lower shelves, reserving the top shelf for objects to be rakued or pieces with overglaze decorations. When the interior of the kiln becomes bright red (about cone 018), we put on asbestos gloves, lift off the kiln top, and with tongs remove the entire top shelf and place it on a layer of insulating brick, then put the top of the kiln back in place. The pieces for raku were put into our raku can, and the overglaze ware was left on the hot shelf to slow down its cooling.

SAFETY PRECAUTIONS

• Don't get burned. Use asbestos gloves when opening a top-loading kiln.

• Be especially careful to use asbestos gloves and tongs that are in good condition when doing raku work. (Let's not drop any red-hot pieces on the floor or the feet!)

• Check the electric cord that plugs your kiln into the house current. Such cords will not live forever, and at the first sign of wear they should be replaced.

• When firing an electric kiln do not operate any other electrical appliances on the same circuit at the same time.

• Avoid the danger of injuries to the eyes by wearing sunglasses when peering through the peephole.

• Make sure there is ample insulation underneath your kiln—cement blocks or firebricks are best.

chapter 13

DECORATING

WE CAN DECORATE our miniature clay creations in any number of ways. One of the most simple forms of decoration is putting a clay of one color on top of a clay of a different color. This can be done by slip trailing.

SLIP TRAILING

This must be done when the clay object is still moist. Using the slip trailer that we saw in Photo Series 24, we can trail a design with white slip on an object made of red clay.

We found that this is most difficult to control in miniature work, and we achieved better results by using a fine brush and painting the slip onto the red-clay object. The box shown in Photo Series 7 was decorated in this manner.

Another way in which slip can be trailed is to use the top of an empty white glue bottle that has a very tiny opening. Have the slip a bit thicker than normal, and squeeze the slip out as you trail it into a design. An advantage of this top is that the cap can be shut tightly so that the slip doesn't dry out when not in use.

For very minute slip designs, trail the slip from "blobs" of slip with a pointed toothpick or a needle. Plate 13-1 shows a box lid that was decorated in this manner.

ENGOBE

This is just another term for slip, but it is frequently used to describe slips that become glazes when they are fired. In other words, some slips are self-glazing engobes.

SGRAFFITO

Sgraffito is scratching through something. If we put a white engobe on top of a red-clay body, then scratch a design in it so that the red color shows through, we are using sgraffito. The bottom part of the box shown in plate 13-1 was decorated by the sgraffito method.

PLATE 13-1

STENCILS AND MASKS

Designs may be cut out of wax paper, laid on ware, and then a design may be dabbed through the stencil with a sponge. Thus on a white-clay body, designs could be made in colored engobe, or white engobe could be dabbed onto a colored-clay body.

Masking is the reverse of stenciling. A shape cut out of wax paper is laid on the ware, and then a sponge is used to dab contrasting color around the mask.

Using engobes this way we must be careful to see to it that the piece is moist or leather hard (not bone dry).

Stencils and masks can also be used to apply overglaze colors to pieces that have been fired and glazed.

Plate 13-2 shows two dinner plates that were cast in a mold. The shape of a butterfly was cut out of wax paper with tiny embroidery scissors. The butterfly cutout was used as a mask, and the paper from which the butterfly was cut became a stencil.

PLATE 13-2

The tiny size presented some difficulties; the butterflies were stubborn and would not stay put on the ware, but came up with the brush or the sponge. The problem was solved by sticking them in place with gum solution. The area around the mask was spattered. A flat square paintbrush was dipped into overglaze colors, pointed at the piece, and then a knife blade was drawn through the bristles away from the ware (the plate shown in the lower portion of the picture).

The stencil was fastened to the plate shown in the upper portion of the picture, and the artist used her finger to dab the overglaze color into the open portion of the stencil. When the stencil was lifted off, the artist discovered that some of the overglaze color had seeped under the edge of the stencil slightly. This turned out to be one of those "happy accidents" that actually made the design more attractive. The antennae of the butterfly were painted on with a brush.

Overglaze colors must be fired at low temperatures, so these pieces received their last firing at about cone 017. Our kiln was to be fired to cone 05, so we used the method described in chapter 12: we put them on a tile and lifted the tile out when the interior of the kiln became a bright red.

MAJOLICA

This is a method of painting a design with underglaze colors on a glazed surface before the glaze has been fired. The piece may be bisqued (fired unglazed) first, or it may be unfired greenware. The glaze is put on the piece, then a thin coat of gum is either sprayed or brushed on top of the glaze, then underglaze pigments are used to paint the design over the glaze. The Majolica method is not limited to brushwork—sponge and stencil can be used as well. There is a special quality to Majolica work brought about by the fact that as the glaze matures underneath the decoration it sometimes alters the design. If the glaze contains a chemical (colemanite, for example) that makes it bubble during the fire, this bubbling will give a distinctive texture to the decoration.

The ornaments shown in the last picture in Photo Series 23 are examples of Majolica (see color section).

WAX RESIST

In this method of decoration the artist paints a design with liquid-wax emulsion on a piece of bisqued (fired) ware, then puts a glaze or an engobe over the entire piece either by brushing or dipping. The waxed surface repels the engobe or the glaze, so that after firing, the design that was brushed on with wax shows the color of the clay. The tops of the towers of the castle shown in plate 6-2 were decorated in this manner. Wax resist was also used in glazing the toothpick holder made by Dorothy Shank in Photo Series 9.

UNDERGLAZE PAINTING

As the name implies, this is a method of painting designs on ware before it is glazed. The ware may be either bisque, or unfired greenware. Underglaze colors are used. We have found that prepared underglaze pigments that can be bought from dealers in complete palettes make the job easier for the miniaturist.

OVERGLAZE PAINTING

This method, sometimes referred to as china painting, involves painting designs on ware that has been glazed and fired. Overglaze pigments, as we mentioned earlier, are fired at a much lower temperature than underglaze colors—usually to cone 018 or cone 017. At this low temperature it is possible to obtain brilliant shades of red (most reds disappear at high-fired temperatures) and also gold and lusters.

chapter · 14

L'ENVOI

NOW THAT we have seen their work, let's find out what the artists have to say about it. In the following pages we shall chat with a number of our old friends and half a dozen new ones, discussing methods and philosophies—exploring what they think and what they feel about working with clay, especially clay miniatures. Some of the interviews were in person, some by mail, and some by telephone. They are arranged in alphabetical order.

Plate 14–1

Irene Batt *(photo by Miles Batt)*

Irene became a potter sixteen years ago when she was vacationing in North Carolina (there are lots of potters in that state). As she wandered through the town she saw a man working on a potter's wheel in his backyard and asked him if she could try it. He laughed at her naïveté and said, "Sure, here's some clay. See what you can do with it."

We can't say that a miracle happened, that Irene threw the clay on the wheel and immediately formed a pot, but since she had the makings of a highly skilled craftsperson, she impressed the potter to such an extent that when she asked him to give her a few lessons, he agreed enthusiastically. Within a couple of days she knew how to throw clay on the wheel and had become committed to a new career, one that turned out to be highly successful and rewarding.

Today Irene Batt, who lives in south Florida, is recognized as a foremost ceramic artist. Her creations appear in public buildings, in banks, and in many private collections in this country and abroad.

She recently finished designing, making, and installing 600 sq. ft. of floor tiles in a deluxe home—the Batt residence—that was designed by the Batts with the aid of architect Donald Singer. It is a home that is a showcase for Irene's ceramics and fiber sculptures and for her husband Miles's paintings.

PLATE 14-1

Unlike the other artists in this book, Irene Batt works almost entirely on a large scale; but she made the mini-candelabrum and mirror for us because she welcomed the challenge to work small.

Irene takes time out occasionally to teach at the Broward Community College and at the Fort Lauderdale Museum because she finds that teaching sharpens her awareness, feeds her imagination, and revitalizes her creative juices.

While we were chatting one day in Irene's studio, we asked her what she thought of modern trends in ceramics:

"It depends upon what you mean by modern," she said. "The term is subjective. Certainly, it involves discovery and inventiveness. When we look at a piece we ask ourselves, Is there enough there to hold one's attention? Does it make a statement?"

"Do you equate contemporary with modern, Irene?"

"No, we can take things from the past, but unless we invent something to go along with our adaptation, then we are not adapting, we are just stealing."

We mentioned the late Charles Harder, professor of ceramics at Alfred University, who used to say when referring to a student's work that showed fine craftsmanship, "That looks as if it had been made on purpose." High praise indeed from Harder.

Then we discussed Irene's visit to one of the most prestigious potters of America during which he advised a young hopeful to throw a great big bowl on the wheel, then slam it on the floor and bang it with a two-by-four—something that would not have met with Harder's approval. We asked if it met with her approval:

"A board banging is a one-time happening," she said. "The question is, Will it hold? There can be discovery in action—making something that will attract attention. Funk art taken from Magritte and other surrealists cannot be compared with sculpture."

Then we referred to a pocket book or a pair of tennis shoes made of clay:

"That is a kind of trompe l'oeil, it fools the eye. I enjoy seeing examples of this."

"What do you think about functional art?"

"We cannot compare functional and funky. We need more functionalism which produces good form. Functional art creates its own form. What is important to keep in mind is that creativity is discovery and invention."

We love a discussion like this and could have carried on all day, but Irene is a busy artist and we had kept her away from her wheel long enough.

Plate 14-2

Charlie Brown

Charlie Brown is a remarkable person. Seventeen years ago at the age of 58 he retired from the business world. Today, after two decades, he has achieved international fame as a major American ceramist. He does not use a potter's wheel; all of his creations are hand built. Until recently most of his work has been done on a large scale. Now he is still making enormous pots, but he is also busily turning out miniatures. Here is what he says about this new facet of his work:

"John, when you asked me six months ago to make a tiny pot, you really got me started on something. Since that day I have made several hundred."

"Your miniatures are quite popular, Charlie; I understand that collectors are eager to buy practically all the mini-pots you make."

"That's true, John; there is a big demand for them. This Christmas one collector decorated his Christmas tree entirely with ceramic miniatures. I take great pleasure in making tiny things; the work goes so rapidly. Just join two bowl shapes to form a ball, make an opening, add a neck, and—presto, in just a few moments you have made a mini-vase. And yet, no matter how many you make, no two will be exactly alike."

"How did you get started in clay, Charlie?"

"I was working as an accountant, but all my life I had been interested

PLATE 14-2

in art and design. I used to be a Sunday painter. In 1951 a friend suggested I enter an evening class in clay sponsored by the University of Florida—I did, and got hooked. It was love at first touch; the way clay responds to the hand and the mind captured my heart. I never painted again. Eleven years later I quit my job to become a full-time potter."

"How do you feel about working small after doing so much large work?"

"John, a tiny creation can have as much beauty and good design as a large one. It all depends upon the energy and the love that is put into it. I am still eager to try new things, still climbing to the top of my mountain, but I doubt that I will ever reach it because—from the summit, where else can one go?"

Plate 14-3

Chris Clark *(photo by Ed Arrowood)*

Chris majored in physical education in college and for a while taught at M.I.T. in Boston where she was director of the women's athletic program. She started taking pottery classes through their student art association and since then has attended numbers of ceramic workshops, but most of her work has been done on her own. At present she is affiliated with Castle Clay in Denver, Colorado, a pottery co-op where she teaches.

She exhibits regularly in Colorado and other western and midwestern states. Her pottery is sold through many stores in Colorado. Chris talks about her work:

"I make castles because it's fun. I get a kick out of imagining little

PLATE 14-3

beings using the towers. I like to put little doors in places where you can't see them unless the piece is broken. A special surprise for someone sometime.

"The whole idea of little castles came from some underwater movies I saw of scuba divers swimming through sunken ships, and it seemed as though it might be fun to make little structures for goldfish to swim in and out of—and then some as terrariums with clay dragons guarding the entrances, and then a fountain with a moat with dry ice foaming and bubbling in it. You can see how your mind goes from one idea to the next. The trick is not to let yourself stop and think 'this is silly,' but to just keep going and let yourself do what brings a smile to your stomach.

"I make functional pottery to keep myself in groceries, etc.; mini-castles are special things that can't be done with any kind of pressure on. They can only 'happen' on a few days when things feel special. They can't be mass-produced or I'm sure they'd lose their uniqueness and the fun would go away.

"The pieces are thrown first. I like to use different clay bodies for different types of castles—porcelain is white and airy, stoneware is more for dark foresty-type castles, terra-cotta for rustic ones. Once the clay sets up some, I can cut out the windows, flute the roofs, attach little doors and hinges, arrange and put the turrets on—this is the most fun—and add passageways and balconies, hidden garden areas, flaming dragons, etc. It's probably a release for a frustrated architect of earlier lives hiding in my bones."

We are grateful to you, Chris, for the smiles you have brought to our stomachs!

Plate 14-4

Dong Hee Suh

We learned about the talented Korean artist Dong Hee Suh through the National Cone Box Show at the University of Kansas. Dong Hee Suh says this about working small, "It's for me! Working small is the way of getting into work and the way of getting variety, quantity, and quality."

PLATE 14-4

Plate 14-5

Frank Eliscu

Frank Eliscu, past president of the National Sculpture Society, is an academician of the National Academy of Design.

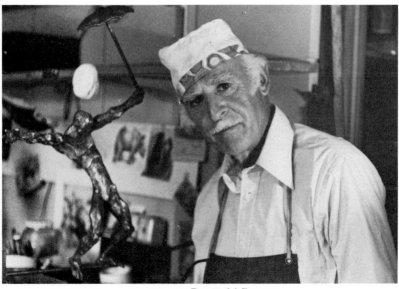

PLATE 14-5

He has won many honors and awards. Among his recent commissions have been *St. Christopher* for the St. Christopher Chapel in New York City; a three-figure sculpture of the astronauts at the Headly Museum, Lexington, Kentucky; *The Torah,* Temple Sinai, Tenafly, New Jersey; *The Naiad* in the lobby of 100 Church Street, New York City; *Man and Atom,* Ventura, California; and many, many others. His *Shark Diver* is in the magnificent Brookgreen Gardens in South Carolina.

Eliscu is the creator of what is probably the best-known piece of sculpture in America—the All-American Football Trophy, popularly known as the *Heisman Trophy.*

Mr. Eliscu is the author of three books on sculpture: *Sculpture— Three Techniques; Direct Wax Sculpture;* and *Slate and Soft Stone Sculpture.*

Plate 14-6

Eleanor Madonik *(photo by Vina Schemer)*

___

Eleanor Madonik has a special feeling about small objects:

"When I was a little girl I had an aunt who kept a magic box filled with tiny treasures. Every birthday I received one. I am still thrilled by tiny treasures, but now I make them, for myself and for others. My daughter, Marcia, is also a potter and was my first pupil."

"How did you become interested in ceramics, Eleanor?"

"After I received my bachelor of fine arts in design from Ohio State University, I studied with Rhoda Lopez in Ann Arbor, Michigan. She gave me a list of tools I would need to become a potter, and at the head of the list was your book on pottery making."

"Tell me about your teaching career."

"I taught for the Cleveland public school system for ten years, primarily in an enrichment art program. After moving to Jacksonville I taught a year in the elementary art program. When I teach I feel an inner resonance—I want the children to sense my excitement. As they made things out of clay, my pupils learned things about technology, chemistry, and the physical sciences. They became interested in glaze, they learned about glass as a supercooled fluid (no crystals), and discovered that old glass is wavy because over the years it slumps. They acquired a scientific vocabulary, became familiar with such terms as eutectics, coefficient of expansion, deliquescence, etc. I showed them how to throw on the wheel: to me that is like dancing—feeling the clay move upward. Centering and opening is balance and leverage."

"Did your pupils work on the wheel?"

"They tried it. Some managed to succeed; a few continued their pottery work when they went on to high school. Now my teaching is done in Florida."

PLATE 14-6

"Let's talk a bit about your ceramic miniatures. Those shown in plate 3-4 are beautiful. How do you form them?"

"I throw off the hump, starting with about 10 lbs. of clay, shape pieces, then cut them off with a nylon fishing line. I make the lids first, then the pots to fit them. The figurines, of course, I model freehand. My miniatures are fired in the range of cone 6 to cone 10."

"That ornate piece of ceramics shown beside you in your portrait is fascinating, and so is the pendant you are wearing. How do you get ideas for your designs?"

"I keep a pad of paper and a pencil on my bedside table. Frequently during the night I wake up and jot down a thought that has come to me."

"Eleanor, you are becoming well known for your ceramics, but I believe you have made even greater achievements, intangible ones, that cannot be hung in galleries or sold in the marketplace. These are the inspirations you have given to young people of all ages."

Plate 14-7

Christie Rogers *(photo by Vina Schemer)*

Christie says this about working in miniatures:

"I have always been interested in tiny things. As a child I preferred very small dolls and stuffed toys. I still have a collection of tiny glass and porcelain animals that I started when I was in grade school. I have many of my small things displayed in an antique-type drawer.

"About four years ago I was in Vina Schemer's class in the Jacksonville Art Museum. She started an informal contest of 'who can make the smallest.' I have enjoyed throwing miniatures since then.

PLATE 14-7

"Besides being something I like doing, miniature making fulfills several other purposes for me. I do a lot of demonstrating around the community. People are fascinated by seeing a little pot grow from a little lump of clay. A miniature can be made fairly quickly and many can be thrown from a small amount of clay.

"Miniatures fill still another purpose for me. I believe that people who are somewhat 'afraid' of crafts can be attracted by the miniature. Perhaps they feel intimidated by 'art,' but through miniatures they can learn to appreciate a growing number of crafts.

"A final purpose for my miniatures is to put handcrafted ceramics in almost anyone's price range. I have been known to drastically reduce the price on a miniature for a small girl with a fist full of change!"

Plate 14-8

Vina Schemer

"Vina, I know that you throw large pieces on the wheel; do you have a special feeling about miniatures?"

"Yes indeed, John. Making something tiny is quite different from making something that is enormous. Accidents are sometimes good on big work, but never on little. In making minis there is a need for precision—there must be perfection. Potters who make large pieces should make small pieces now and then just to remind them of the importance of the delicate touch and of fine craftsmanship.

"In my pottery classes for adults I now and then challenge the students to make minis—let them see what they can do with scrapings left on the wheel head. One or two of them succeed. But succeed or not, the experience helps."

185

PLATE 14-8

PLATE 14-8

Vina has collected miniatures since her childhood days. She herself is a delightful miniature, five feet tall.

Plate 14-9

Sandra McKenzie Schmitt *(photo by Charles Klabunde)*

Sandra has been living and working in New York City for the past twelve years. Galleries in New York, New Jersey, Connecticut, Pennsylvania, and Florida, as well as museum shops, sell her creations. Despite this she still considers herself a folk artist.

PLATE 14-9

Sandra received her B.A. in 1961 from Lindenwood College for Women, after that she studied at the Universities of Illinois and Wisconsin. She earned her M.A. at the University of Iowa.

She has received many honors and awards.

Sandra's work is an idyllic memory of a happy childhood spent in a small town in Illinois. When she speaks of it she recalls summer evenings when the family sat on the front porch or in the yard while children rode bicycles or played games until bedtime. "Everybody went to town on Wednesday and Saturday evenings," she says, "for shopping, for conversation, and to eat popcorn and ice-cream cones."

Sandra has captured in her tiny sculptures of cityscapes, houses, farms, and cottages the beauty of that rural childhood. It is obvious that her miniatures are a work of love.

Incidentally, Charles Klabunde who took the above photo is an artist of note and also Sandra's husband.

Plate 14-10

Dorothy Ann Shank *(photo by Lee Shank)*

Dorothy graduated from the Ringling School of Art in Sarasota, Florida, with a degree in interior design, and she worked as an interior designer for many years.

Her first instruction in pottery came from our good friend Charlie Brown in Mandarin, Florida, in 1969. She and her husband, Lee, went into full-time pottery production in 1972. Their studio is an old railroad depot and an old country store in Reddick, Florida.

This husband and wife team have a special feeling for clay. Things they make are so appealing that one just has to pick them up and fondle them. Their toothpick holders shown in the color section are so delightful to hold that one might wish that they were goblets to drink from. (After all, who said they *must* hold only toothpicks?)

PLATE 14-10

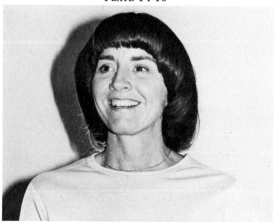

Plate 14-11

David Snair (*photo by Susan Martin*)
_____

On the cover of the December 1975 issue of *Ceramics Monthly* magazine was a fascinating picture of a crystalline-glazed porcelain bottle. We wondered if David had ever made any miniature vases with similar glazes and wrote to ask him. It turned out that his interest in miniature ceramics is just as strong as ours. The four miniature porcelain vases shown in the color section were thrown by David on a potter's wheel and were glazed with formulas he created himself.

PLATE 14-11

Through our correspondence with David we learned that he and his partner, Dawn King, are the owners of the firm *Environmental Porcelain* (fine porcelain as jewelry for living spaces) in Newbury Park, California.

David writes about his work as follows:

"I started making miniature vases to use as test tiles while a graduate student at Purdue. They were a fantastic solution to a number of problems. We had several large kilns on a very crowded firing schedule, limited clay-making equipment, and a strong interest in glazes on my part. I could easily make a hundred or so mini-bowls in an hour or two out of very little clay, fit them into kiln space that was otherwise wasted, and end up with a lot of really beautiful (and saleable) pieces. I always hate making "normal" test tiles which seldom tell how a glaze works anyhow.

"Most of the crystalline pieces I made at first were quite large— disasters abounded! Time to form, trim, etc. was about an hour, and literally hundreds were failures and ended up as, heaven knows, how many trash cans of shards.

"Then I started making miniature bottles—at first, just as 'test tiles,' then they became things of their own. The small scale seemed more akin to what I was trying to produce—a sort of synthesis of many of the elements I find in nature, consisting of flowers, seedpods, minerals, shells, etc. I find there are forms, colors, and patterns, and combinations of these exist—or at least work best only as miniatures. There is also a challenge. If a miniature works, it fits into a hand, it belies its size and takes on an apparent size and importance much beyond its physical dimensions. If it fails, it's a misshapen little lump."

Plate 14-12

Dee Snyder

Dee Snyder seems to belong to the miniature world. She lives in a house surrounded by fine porcelains she has collected and also surrounded by dollhouses and miniature corner rooms that she and her husband have created.

Dee majored in journalism in college with a minor in fine arts. She studied interior design and painting and has exhibited in galleries in the Palm Beach, Florida, area where she lives.

At present Dee teaches miniature making. She is president of Lake House Studio, Inc., which produces custom miniatures for collectors; she is associate editor of *Nutshell News,* a bimonthly magazine for miniaturists; she is coauthor, with Catherine B. MacLaren, of *This Side of Yesterday in Miniature,* published in 1975, and writes articles for magazines on miniature making. Dee participated in a seminar on Oriental ceramics at Oxford University in September, 1979.

PLATE 14-12

This photograph shows Dee Snyder holding one of the favorite pieces in her collection, an antique French hare terrine. The reproduction of this in miniature is in Dee's "Kitchen Corner" (plate 6-13) on the table just in front of the cook.

Plate 14-13

Evelyn Strid

Evelyn Strid is the mother of the proprietor of a store that sells toys and dollhouses for children and miniature furnishings for dollhouse aficionados. The store, called Poppenhuizen, is in Philadelphia. A year or so ago her son and daughter-in-law got her so interested in what they were doing that she decided to open her own Poppenhuizen in her hometown of Delray Beach.

Business is brisk. Besides selling commercially manufactured furnishings, Evelyn serves as a consultant on dollhouse interior decoration.

PLATE 14-13

In this photograph she is shown holding a sort of pyramidal étagère that displays four of her room designs (this is only ½" = 1' scale; often times Evelyn finds a collector who prefers the smaller scale models.) Evelyn made all of the items shown in the étagère except the love seat on the first floor.

Her first experience with clay came a short time ago when she found difficulty in keeping up with demands of her customers for dishes for dollhouses (especially for the Quimper ware that is one of her specialties). She has had no formal training in ceramics, but she is a born artist. So all she had to do was read a good book, buy a small kiln, some clay, and tools, and get to work.

In her words, "Once you become involved in miniature work, you become completely absorbed—and it is *so* relaxing."

Plate 14-14

Chris Unterseher (*photo by Ted Cook*)

PLATE 14-14

Chris Unterseher, associate professor of art at the University of Nevada, has had a distinguished career as an artist and as a teacher.

To list all of the shows in which his work has been displayed, the schools where he has taught and lectured, the private collections that include his work, and the write-ups he has received in books and periodicals would take six full pages.

Among awards he has won are first prize, Arizona Craftsmen Exhibition, Flagstaff, Arizona, 1973; purchase prize, Annual Graphic Competition, Reno, Nevada, 1971; purchase award, Second Annual Juried Art Exhibition, University of California, Davis, California, 1968.

He has had fifteen one-man shows in the last eleven years. One of these, the Haute Porcelaine Exhibition in the Wenger Gallery in San Francisco, 1973, must receive special mention. Says Chris, "The Haute Porcelaine Show was really my first attempt to work in miniature. My creations have always been small, but in this show I had more than two dozen pieces, none over 4″ x 4″ in size. All of them documenting architecture and objects of the Art Deco period."

Plate 14-15

Carla and John

When we sold our home in Mexico where we had lived for many years, we left our studio behind and moved to a small apartment. We were asked to write a book on miniature ceramics, and we wondered if that could be done in the corner of our living room. It was a challenge. We tried it and found fulfillment as well as pleasure. We learned too that some of the new friends we made in this field work in studios no bigger than ours.

A WORD ABOUT THE AUTHORS

Our paths have crisscrossed a good many times in the course of thirty-eight years. Each intersection still glows from some discovery induced by that relentless Kenny capacity for the enjoyment of their own discoveries—a new medium or process, a fascinating historical connection, a clever way to solve an old problem, the sense of "Hey, I'd like to try my hand at that!"

Carla and John are true collectors—gatherers of friends and experiences, rather than possessions, of checked-out know-how, as against blind expenditures. They live modestly, in the sun where the ocean licks the land. They travel much, and often, and far—and light. The Kennys are at home in museums, castles, cathedrals, and libraries around the world feathering their nest with souvenirs and reproductions. They are teachers in the fullest sense, sharing their insights and productivity with all who care to benefit. Their lessons live in the countless careers and creativity of their students and their readers.

On a stormy morning recently the manuscript for this the eighth Kenny book lay ready for the editor. John, up early at his desk facing the

PLATE 14-15

Atlantic, rose and walked across the room in search of a suitable envelope, when with an explosive supersonic boom the wall-size picture window blew in, shooting a hail of glass shards across the desk and most of the room. By a split-second miracle John and Carla and the manuscript escaped unharmed.

Now a great many new readers will come to know the infectious Kenny enthusiasm, focused this time on ceramics in miniature. While the Kennys are waiting for their boarded-up window to be reglazed, they are also getting ready to set sail (on a freighter) in search of their next topic. I suppose it's safe to predict it will not be about glass or plywood. But then you never can tell. Experience is, after all, the greatest teacher of all!

Tom Naegele
High School of Art & Design
New York, N.Y.

APPENDIX

DETERMINING THE PERCENTAGES OF ELECTROLYTES NEEDED TO DEFLOCCULATE CLAY

1. Mix together 1,000 grams of dry clay and 400 grams of water.
2. Put 25 cc. of water in a glass graduate, and add 3 grams of soda ash and 3 grams of sodium silicate. (To weigh sodium silicate, put the graduate containing water on a scale and weigh it. Add sodium silicate drop by drop until the total weight of container and solution increases to the desired amount.) Then add enough water to bring the quantity up to 30 cc.
3. Add the solution to the clay drop by drop, while stirring the clay constantly.
4. When the clay turns into a liquid thin enough to pour, consult the graduate to find out how much of the solution has been used.
5. Calculate as follows:

$$\frac{\text{Number of grams of solution used}}{100} = \text{percent of each deflocculant required.}$$

Note 1: Don't go wrong on a decimal here. If it required 15 grams of the solution to make the clay liquid, then $15/100 = 0.15$, so it takes 0.15 percent of soda ash and 0.15 percent of sodium silicate to deflocculate the clay.

Note 2: If clay does not turn liquid add additional amounts of water, but not enough to make the total weight of water more than 500 grams (50 percent of clay content). If this does not work, try substituting different electrolytes, sal soda, sodium tannate, sodium alginate, or a commercial water softener such as Calgon.

Note 3: Some clays are impossible to deflocculate.

TABLE OF CONE TEMPERATURES

Cone	Centi-grade	Fahren-heit	Color of Fire	What Happens to Clay	Type of Ware and Glazes
15	1435	2615			
14	1400	2552			
13	1350	2462		porcelain	porcelain
12	1335	2435		matures	
11	1325	2417			
10	1305	2381	white		china bodies
9	1285	2345		stoneware clays	stoneware
8	1260	2300		mature	salt glazes
7	1250	2282			
6	1230	2246			
5	1205	2201			
4	1190	2174		red clays melt	china glazes
3	1170	2138			
2	1165	2129			semivitreous ware
1	1160	2120			
01	1145	2093	yellow		
02	1125	2057		buff clays	earthenware
03	1115	2039		mature	
04	1060	1940			
05	1040	1904			
06	1015	1859		red clays mature	
07	990	1814			low-fired earthenware
08	950	1742	orange		
09	930	1706			low-fired lead glazes
010	905	1661			
011	895	1643	cherry red		
012	875	1607			lustre glazes
013	860	1580			
014	830	1526			
015	805	1481		organic matter in	chrome red glazes
016	795	1463		clay burns out	
017	770	1418	dull red		
018	720	1328			overglaze colors
019	660	1220			enamels
020	650	1202			
021	615	1139			
022	605	1121		dehydration begins	

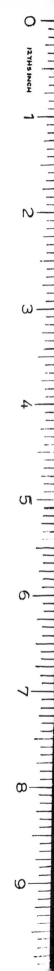

RULER: *Scale for miniatures in 1/12″*

Periodicals Recommended for the
Ceramic Miniaturist

Ceramics Monthly
Box 12448
Columbus, OH 43212
The complete magazine for the ceramic artist.

Collector Editions Quarterly
170 Fifth Avenue
New York, NY 10010

Doll Castle News
P.O. Box 247
Washington, NJ 07882

The Enchanted Dollhouse
Manchester Center, VT 05255

Miniature Collector
12 Queen Anne Place
Marion, OH 43302

Miniature World
P.O. Box 337
Seabrook, NH 03874

Nutshell News (also *The Miniatures Catalog*)
Clifton House
Clifton, VA 22024

The Scale Cabinetmaker
P.O. Box 87
Pembroke, VA 24136

This magazine has a Dealer Directory as well as a Workshop Directory.

Sources of Supplies

Because of changes in addresses, we have listed those suppliers we are familiar with and whose addresses have remained constant for some time. However, there are many, many more whose supplies will most surely serve your needs; therefore, in order to keep up-to-date we suggest you check some of the many craft magazines that have current listings of suppliers of ceramic equipment—tools, clays, and kilns.

It is recommended that you write to find out if a catalog is available, if it is free, etc. Be sure to enclose a self-addressed, stamped envelope to ensure a prompt reply. Learn about *sample kits*—we found these perfect for making ceramic miniatures.

Check the Yellow Pages for ceramic craft centers in your area, and see what they may have in the way of supplies, equipment, and firing schedules. And don't forget the many tools you have at hand in your kitchen and your sewing or crochet kit.

American Art Clay Company
(AMACO)
4717 W. Sixteenth Street
Indianapolis, IN 46222

Clay, glazes, tools, kilns.

The Dollhouse
176 Ninth Avenue
New York, NY 10011

Complete collection of materials
for do-it-yourself miniature
dollhouse enthusiasts.

Duncan Ceramic Products
P.O. Box 7827
Fresno, CA 93727

Glazes, tools, kilns.

Cir-Kit Concepts, Inc.
612 North Broadway
Rochester, MN 55901

Lighting specialists for the
miniaturists. Special detailed
instruction booklet.

Illinois Hobbycraft
12 S. Fifth Street
Geneva, IL 60134

Electrical wiring kits for
miniature rooms and dollhouses.

Kemper Tools, Kemper Mfg. Inc.
P.O. Box 545
Chino, CA 91710

Fine tools for the ceramic
craftsman.

Mayco Colors
20800 Dearborn Street
Chatsworth, CA 91311

Glazes.

Mini D'Lights
P.O. Drawer 398
Staten Island, NY 10304

Lighting accessories for
chandeliers, sconces, and
candlesticks. Mini-candles,
candle-flame bulbs, transformers,
etc.

Miniland
1799 State Road 7
Margate, Fort Lauderdale, FL
33063

A complete miniature shop—
accessories, collectors' items.

Mini Mundus
970 Lexington Avenue
New York, NY 10021

Everything for the miniaturist—
tools, accessories, materials,
patterns, publications.

Nova Kilns, Thermolyne Corp.
Subsidiary of Sybron Corp.
2555 Kerper Boulevard
Dubuque, IA 52001

Kilns for the miniaturist.

The Edward Orton, Jr., Ceramic   Pyrometric cones and cone
Foundation   plaques.
1445 Summit Street
Columbus, OH 43201

Seeley's Ceramic Service, Inc.   Tools, equipment, molds, for doll
9 River Street   making, and special small kilns
Oneonta, NY 13820   for dolls and miniatures in
                                      porcelain.

SNO Industries   Ceramic and porcelain kilns.
Route 130 & Lincoln Avenue
P.O. Box Ephraim, NJ 08059

Teka Fine Line Brushes, Inc.   Brushes especially made for
3704 Bedford Avenue   miniature work.
Brooklyn, NY 11229

WCS Pottery Equipment &   Clay.
Supplies
14400 Lomitas Avenue
Dept. B027
Industry, CA 91746

X-Acto   Tools for the miniaturist.
45-35 Van Dam Street
Long Island City, NY

Fountains:

Ace Pump Co.
57 W. Twenty-first Street
New York, NY 10010

Canal Electric Motors
310 Canal Street
New York, NY 10013

Hall Fountains, Inc.
5500 N.W. Twenty-second Avenue
Fort Lauderdale, FL 33309

Little Giant Pump Co.
3810 N. Tulsa Street
Oklahoma City, OK 73112

GLOSSARY

CERAMIC TERMS

Adobe—A clay found in desert regions. It can be used as slip.

Albany slip—A natural clay that melts at cone 8. Used as a glaze on clay that fires at a higher temperature. Usually dark brown. Used by Early American potters on stoneware, and used today on porcelain electrical insulators.

Alkali—Any substance having marked basic properties. For potters the term refers generally to compounds of sodium and potassium that act as fluxes in alkaline glazes.

Amorphous—Formless. In chemistry it refers to a lack of crystalline structure.

Argillaceous—Of the nature of clay or containing clay.

Armature—A framework used to support clay while it is being modeled.

Arretine ware—Red terra-cotta, decorated in relief, and made at Arretium in Italy, from about 100 B.C. to about A.D. 100.

Aventurine—A glossy type of glaze containing sparkling particles of copper or chromic oxide or ferric oxide.

Banding wheel (also **whirler** or **decorating wheel**)—A turntable that permits work to be rotated while it is shaped or decorated.

Basalt ware—A type of black stoneware developed by Josiah Wedgwood.

Bat—A disc or slab of plaster of paris or fired clay used to dry out clay or to work on.

Bentonite—A clay of volcanic origin that is used to make clay bodies more plastic. Always mixed with other dry ingredients.

Bisque—Unglazed fired clay.

Blanks—Pottery shapes, tiles, plates, fired but not glazed, used for applied decorations.

Bone china—Hard translucent whiteware containing bone ash (calcium phosphate). Originally produced in England.

Burnishing—Producing a shiny surface on clay by rubbing it with a smooth tool when it is leather hard.

Calcareous—Containing lime.

Calcining—A process of firing a material to expel volatile matter and to dehydrate it; done frequently with clay, borax, and other material before they are used in glaze recipes.

Calipers—A device for measuring the dimensions of objects.

Calipers, proportional—A device for enlarging or reducing dimensions proportionately.

Case mold—A mold from which other molds are made.

Casting—The process of pouring a liquid, either slip or plaster of paris, into a mold where it hardens.

Celadon—A pale green glaze produced by iron in a reduction fire.

Cheese state—The period during the setting of plaster of paris when it has the consistency of cream cheese.

Chemically combined water—Water that is combined in molecular form with clay to make it a hydrous aluminum silicate. This water is driven off in the kiln when the clay reaches red heat (about 900° to 1000°F.).

CMC—A synthetic gum for glazes.

Coefficient of expansion—The ratio of increase in size of a substance for a given rise in temperature.

Colloidal—Made up of extremely fine particles suspended in a fluid medium; gelatinous.

Cones, pyrometric—Small clay rods that indicate kiln temperatures.

Cottle—A wall set in place around a model when plaster of paris is to be poured over it.

Crackle—Tiny cracks in the surface of a glaze.

Crawling—A glaze defect in which the glaze rolls away from areas of the piece it is on, leaving bare spots.

Crazing—A glaze defect resulting from lack of fit between a glaze and the body it is on so that fine cracks appear in the glaze.

Crystallization—The formation of crystals. This occurs in glazes containing rutile, zinc, and other crystal-forming oxides.

De-airing—The process of subjecting plastic clay to a vacuum so that most of the air is drawn out of the clay. This makes it better for throwing. A de-airing device is usually attached to a pug mill.

Decalcomania—A process of transferring pictures and designs from specially prepared paper to china or glass.

Decant—To pour off liquid gently without disturbing the solid material that has settled.

Decomposition—The act of separating or resolving into constituent parts; disintegration. It is the decomposition of granite rock that forms clay.

Deflocculation—The addition of electrolytes to clay slip to reduce the amount of water needed to make it pourable.

Dehydration—The expulsion of water. Clay is dehydrated when the chemically combined water is driven off at about 1000°F.

Deliquescence—Process of becoming liquid by absorbing water from the air.

Devitrification—Recrystallization on cooling, which is a defect in glazes.

Dipping—A method of applying glaze to a piece of pottery by immersing it in a container of glaze.

Draft—The taper on the sides of a model that permits it to be withdrawn from a mold.

Dresden china—Decorated porcelain made near Dresden in Saxony that is characterized by elaborate ornamentation and delicate figure pieces. Also called *Meissen ware.*

Dry footing—The process of removing glaze from the bottom rim of a piece so that it can be fired standing on a kiln shelf without stilts.

Earthenware—Pottery fired to a temperature below 2000°F.

Electrolyte—An alkaline substance, usually soda ash or sodium silicate, added to a clay slip to deflocculate it.

Engobe—Clay slip, usually colored.

Epoxy cement—A strong adhesive good for attaching tiles to masonry walls.

Extruding—Process of shaping plastic clay by forcing it through a die.

Faience—Earthenware covered with opaque glaze, with decorations painted over the glaze.

Fat clay—Clay that is highly plastic.

Fettling—Removing the seams (fettles) of a cast piece.

Filler—A nonplastic material, such as flint, added to clay bodies to help drying and control shrinkage.

Filter press—A device for squeezing water out of clay slip to make the slip into plastic clay.

Fit—The adjustment between a glaze and the clay that it is on.

Flux—A substance that melts and also causes other substances to melt.

Frit—A glaze or partial glaze that has been fired and pulverized.

Frog—A device for cutting clay made by a wire stretched across two prongs.

Fuse—To melt under the action of heat.

Glass—An amorphous substance, usually transparent or translucent, made by fusing together silica and soda and some other base.

Glass cullet—Finely pulverized glass used as an ingredient in glazes or as a body flux.

Globar—An electric element in the form of a bar, made of silicon carbide, capable of reaching extremely high temperatures.

Greenware—Clay shapes that have not been fired.

Hard paste—True porcelain.

Igneous—Formed by the solidification of molten masses.

Infrared lamp—A type of electric light bulb whose light is good for drying clay.

Insulating bricks—Extremely porous, soft bricks used on the outside of kilns to reduce the loss of heat through the walls.

Jiggering—The process of manufacturing pottery by means of convex molds and templates on a power wheel.

Kiln furniture—Refractory shelves and posts used to stack a kiln.

Kiln wash—A mixture of china clay and flint with enough water added to make it brushable. Used to protect kiln shelves from glazes that may fall upon them.

Lawn—To pass through a fine mesh screen.

Leaching—Subjecting to the action of percolating water or other liquid in order to separate soluble components.

Luster—A type of surface decoration made by depositing a thin layer of metal.

Luting—The process of joining two pieces of leather-hard clay with slip or slurry.

Majolica—Earthenware covered with an opaque glaze containing tin, with decorations painted on top of the glaze. Named for the island of Majorca.

Mat—Dull surfaced; not shiny.

Maturing—Reaching the temperature that produces the most serviceable degree of hardness. In the case of glaze, reaching the point of complete fusion.

Meissen ware—Dresden china.

Metamorphic—Changed in constitution by heat, pressure, water; said of rocks.

Muffle—A chamber in a kiln that protects ware from contact with the flame.

Nichrome—A chromium nickel alloy used as an element in electric kilns. Limited to temperatures of cone 2 and below.

Notches—Round depressions cut in one half of a mold so that when the other half is cast against it, it will fit in place.

Opacifier—Material added to a transparent glaze to make it opaque; most commonly used are tin oxide and Zircopax.

Organic materials—Vegetable or animal material sometimes present in natural clay.

Oxidation—The act of combining with oxygen, usually at high temperatures.

Parian ware—A fine white translucent porcelain (named for the island of Paros, famed for its beautiful marble).

Patina—A surface appearance on objects, usually the result of age. Ceramic sculpture can be given a patina by treatment with wax, oil, and other materials.

Peeling—A defect in which portions of a glaze or an engobe separate from the ware.

Piercing—Cutting through the wall of a piece to create an open design.

Pinholes—A glaze defect caused by too rapid firing or by tiny air holes in the clay.

Plaster of paris—Partially dehydrated calcium sulfate that is made by calcining gypsum rock. Useful for bats and molds.

Plasticity—A quality of clay that permits it to be molded into different shapes without crumbling or sagging.

Pooled glaze—A fluid glaze that has flowed to the bottom of a bowl, or a depression, forming a pool.

Porcelain—A hard white body, often translucent, composed chiefly of kaolin and feldspar, fired to cone 12 or higher.

Porosity—The quality or degree of being porous, filled with holes, and capable of absorbing liquids.

Pressing—A method of shaping clay by squeezing it into molds or between the two halves of a press mold.

Pugging—Grinding and mixing clay in a pug mill.

Pug mill—A machine for grinding and mixing plastic clay. Usually has a vacuum attached.

Pyrometer—A device for measuring kiln temperature that is usually operated by an electric thermocouple.

Raku—Japanese earthenware used in the tea ceremony. It is rough, with dark glaze.

Raw glaze—A glaze that contains no fritted materials.

Reducing agent—Organic material put in a glaze or into a kiln chamber during the firing to bring about reduction.

Reduction—The act of removing oxygen from metal oxides; occurs during fire when not enough oxygen is present.

Refractory—Resisting high temperatures.

Relief—Sculptural form that projects from a background.

Reticulation—The netlike appearance that frequently occurs when a nonflowing glaze is put on top of one that flows more freely. Also occurs in glazes high in boric oxide.

Rib—A flat tool, usually wood, used to refine shapes being thrown on a potter's wheel.

Salt glazing—A method of glazing ware (usually stoneware) by throwing salt into the firebox of the kiln when temperature is at its highest point.

Sand casting—A method of creating form by pouring a material that will set, such as plaster of paris, cement, or clay slip, into a hollow scooped out of wet sand.

Sang de boeuf—Oxblood, a deep red copper reduction glaze.

Sedimentary—Formed by the deposit of sediment; said of rocks and clays.

Setting—The act of hardening as a result of cooling or chemical action.

Settling—A process by which materials in suspension, such as glazes, fall to the bottom of a container, often forming a hard mass.

Sgraffito—A method of decorating by scratching through a coating of engobe.

Shard—A pottery fragment.

Shims—Pieces of thin material used to separate portions of a mold.

Shivering—A glaze defect in which sections of a glaze lift off the piece.

Short clay—Clay that is not plastic.

Sinter—To harden by heat without reaching maturing temperature.

Slake—To soak with water.

Slip—Liquid clay.

Slurry—Clay of pastelike consistency.

Soft paste—An imitation of porcelain containing various materials, such as gypsum, calcium, bone, which act as fluxes, making the ware mature at a lower temperature than does true porcelain.

Spraying—A method of applying glazes with a spray gun.

Sprig—A relief decoration pressed in a sprig mold attached to ware with slip.

Stacking—Loading a kiln.

Stains—Pigments used for coloring clay bodies and glazes.

Stilts—Porcelain tripods on which glazed ware is fired. Stilts for low-fired work may have points of nichrome.

Stoneware—High-fired vitreous ware, usually gray, sometimes shades of brown or tan.

Temperature—Intensity of heat measured in degrees Fahrenheit or centigrade.

Template—A pattern for shaping the profile of a piece.

Terra-cotta—Low-fired earthenware, usually red, often containing grog, used for sculpture.

Terra sigillata—A surface treatment, developed by the Romans that gives pottery a hard, semiglossy surface. It is made by spraying on an engobe of extremely fine colloidal particles of clay.

Tessera—A small piece of tile, glass, or other hard material used to make mosaics.

Thread separation—A method of separating the two halves of a waste mold by pulling a thread through the plaster when it is in the cheese state.

Tin enamel—A type of low-fire lead glaze containing tin, used in Majolica work.

Trailing—Using a tube to apply a line of slip to clay.

Translucent—Transmitting light but not transparent.

Turntable—A rotating platform on which work may be turned; a banding wheel.

Viscosity—Resistance of a liquid to movement.

Vitrification—The act of becoming vitreous, that is, hard, glasslike, nonabsorbent.

Volatilize—To pass from solid through liquid to gaseous state under the action of heat.

Water smoking—The first portion of the firing cycle during which water is driven from the clay.

Wax resist—A method of decoration in which liquid wax is applied to portions of greenware after which engobe is brushed or sprayed over the piece. The wax repels the engobe.

Weathering—Decomposition under the action of wind, rain, heat, etc.

Wedging—The act of kneading or mixing plastic clay by cutting it in half and slamming the halves together.

CERAMIC MATERIALS

Albany slip—A natural clay that melts to form a deep reddish brown glaze when fired above cone 7. Used on stoneware and on porcelain electrical insulators.

Antimony—A source of color: opaque white in leadless glazes; semi-opaque yellow in lead glazes.

Barium—Barium carbonate ($BaCO_3$). Used in clay bodies to make sulfides insoluble. Used in glazes for mat texture.

Bentonite—A highly plastic, very fine clay of volcanic origin. Used in small quantities to make other clays plastic.

Bone ash—Calcium phosphate ($Ca_3(PO_4)_2$). Added to china clay to produce bone china.

Borax—($Na_2O \cdot 2B_2O_3 \cdot 10H_2O$). Used as a flux in low-temperature glazes. It is highly soluble and therefore almost always used fritted. It produces beautiful colors, especially with copper oxide.

Cadmium—Used with selenium to produce red stains for glazes.

Calcium—An active flux usually used as whiting or calcium carbonate ($CaCO_3$) in glazes and clay bodies.

Ceramispar—Crushed granite used in clay bodies.

Chromium—A source of color when used as chromium oxide (Cr_2O_3). Produces shades of green in lead-free glazes. At extremely low temperatures in lead glazes produces red in an oxidizing fire. Under reduction produces yellow in high-lead glazes. In conjunction with tin oxide produces various shades of pink and maroon.

Cobalt—An important color source that produces a deep blue. Usually used as cobalt carbonate ($CoCO_3$). In combination with copper, manganese, and iron it produces black and gun metal glazes. Sometimes used as cobalt oxide (CoO), which is stronger, or as cobalt nitrate, a soluble salt used to add a slight bluish cast to a glaze or a body.

Colemanite—($2CaO \cdot 3B_2O_3 \cdot 5H_2O$). A natural source of calcium oxide and boric oxide. Used in glazes (called borosilicate glazes).

Copper—An important color source used usually as copper carbonate ($CuCO_3$) or copper oxide (CuO). In a lead glaze produces shades of green. In alkaline glazes produces turquoise blue. In a reduction fire produces colors ranging from purple to brilliant red.

Cornwall stone—A material resembling feldspar. Used as a flux in glazes. As a body ingredient tends to reduce warping.

Crocus martis—A color source producing reddish brown. Contains combinations of iron, oxide, and manganese dioxide.

Cryolite—(Na_3AlF_6). A flux used in enamels and glazes.

Dextrine—A binder for glazes.

Dolomite—($CaMg(CO_3)_2$). A source of magnesium oxide and calcium oxide used to replace part of the whiting in glazes and clay bodies.

Electrolyte—An alkaline substance, usually soda ash or sodium silicate, used to deflocculate clay slip. Other electrolytes include sodium alginate, sal soda, sodium tannate, and some water softeners.

Epsom salts—Used to prevent glazes, especially fritted glazes, from settling.

Fat oil, or **fat oil of turpentine**—A vehicle used in china painting.

Feldspar—In pure form $NaO \cdot Al_2O_3 \cdot 6SiO_2$, or albite. Rarely found in nature as a pure mineral but rather as a mixture of several types of feldspar that contain oxides of sodium, potassium, or calcium. The most important ceramic material next to clay. Used as a flux in clay bodies and in glazes.

Flint—Silica.

Fluorspar—Calcium fluoride (CaF_2). Acts as an opacifier and a flux in glazes.

Frit—A glaze that has been fired and pulverized.

Glass cullet—Pulverized glaze used as a glaze ingredient or as a flux in clay bodies.

Grog—Clay that has been fired and ground. Used in clay bodies to control shrinkage and to give rough texture.

Groleg—An English plastic-porcelain clay with a low shrinkage.

Gums—Binders used in engobes and underglaze decorations as well as in glazes. Most frequently used are gum tragacanth, gum arabic, CMC, V gum T, and various other prepared forms.

Gypsum—A naturally occurring material, hydrated sulfate of calcium ($CaSO_4 \cdot 2H_2O$), which is calcined to make plaster of paris. In its pure form it is called alabaster.

Ilmenite—A titanium compound ($TiO_2 \cdot FeO$). Used in granular form to produce specks in glazes.

Iron—An important source of color in bodies and glazes: in clay bodies produces shades from tan to brick red; in glazes produces shades of yellow, brown, and tan; in a high-lead glaze at low temperature will produce iron red. An extra amount of iron produces a gold-flecked glaze called *aventurine*. In reduction, iron produces the beautiful green glaze *celadon*. Iron has three oxide forms: red (Fe_2O_3), black (FeO), and magnetite (Fe_3O_4).

Iron chromate—($FeCrO_4$). A source of color, especially for clay bodies: produces shades of gray.

Lead—The most widely used flux in low-temperature glazes. Used as lead carbonate ($2PbCO_3 \cdot Pb(OH)_2$) or white lead. Red lead (Pb_3O_4) and litharge (PbO) mixed with molasses have been used to glaze primitive types of low-fired earthenware. Lead chromate ($PbCrO_4$), a source of color, produces shades of green in alkaline glazes and yellow in lead glazes. In the presence of tin it produces shades of pink. POISONOUS.

Lepidolite—($LiF \cdot KF \cdot Al_2O_3 \cdot 3SiO_2$). A flux used in high-fired glazes.

Litharge—Lead monoxide (PbO). Not used as much in ceramics as it is in other sources of lead. POISONOUS.

Magnesite—Magnesium carbonate ($MgCO_3$).

Magnesium—Used as magnesium carbonate ($MgCO_3$) as a flux in high-temperature glazes.

Magnetite—(Fe_3O_4). An oxide of iron.

Manganese—A source of color in glazes and bodies: produces shades of red, brown, purple, and black. Used as manganese carbonate ($MnCO_3$) or as manganese dioxide (MnO_2).

Maroon base—A prepared ceramic pigment made by calcining chromium in the presence of tin.

Nepheline syenite—A type of feldspar with a low fusion point; used in place of other feldspar as a flux in stoneware bodies to lower maturing temperature.

Nickel oxide, green (NiO) or **nickel oxide, black** (Ni_2O_3)—Sources of color in glazes: in the presence of zinc, they produce shades of slate blue; with calcium, shades of tan; with barium, brown; with magnesia, green. Both oxides produce similar results. Useful in crystalline glazes.

Niter—Potassium nitrate (KNO_3). A source of potassium used in making frits.

Ocher—An iron ore used as a colorant for clay bodies to produce shades of yellow, red, or brown.

Opax—A commercial silicate of zirconium. Acts as an opacifier in glazes.

Pearl ash—Potassium carbonate (K_2CO_3). Used as a source of potassium in glazes, usually fritted.

Petuntse—A feldspar found in China. Early Chinese potters mixed it with kaolin to make porcelain.

Pink oxide—*See* Maroon base.

Plaster of paris—Calcium sulfate ($CaSO_4 \cdot \frac{1}{2}H_2O$). Made by calcining gypsum. Used for making molds and casts.

Plasteline—Clay ground with oil so that it becomes nondrying. Used to model forms from which casts are made.

Potassium dichromate—($K_2Cr_2O_3$). A source of color in glazes: produces yellow, red.

Pumicite—An ash formed by volcanic action. A kind of natural frit that can be used as a glaze ingredient.

Rutile—An ore containing titanium dioxide (TiO_2) and iron. Produces light shades of yellow and tan in glazes; also produces broken color and mottled effects; with copper or cobalt it produces beautifully textured colors.

Salt, common—Sodium chloride (NaCl). Produces a hard glaze on stoneware when thrown into the kiln at its highest temperature.

Salts, soluble—Metallic salts such as copper sulfate, silver nitrate, gold chloride, bismuth subnitrate, and others, used to produce lusters. Also used to brush light washes of color over glazes.

Sand—Silica.

Selenium—A source of red in glazes and glaze stains.

Silica (Si) or **flint**—Most abundant substance in the earth's rocky crust. A major component of clays and glazes. Flint is used in glazes to change the coefficient of expansion and to control crazing and shivering.

Silicon carbide—(SiC). Used very finely ground as a reducing agent in glazes; coarse ground it produces lava-type glazes. Also used as an abrasive (carborundum) and an electric-kiln element (Globar).

Size (potter's soap)—A neutral soap manufactured especially for ceramic work that is used as a separator in mold making.

Soapstone—Talc.

Soda—Sodium oxide (Na_2O). An active flux that is useful in glazes, from the lowest to the highest temperature. Has some disadvantages: high coefficient of expansion; glazes are soft, easily scratched. Many feldspars contain soda. Glazes with high-soda content have beautiful colors, especially the turquoise blue produced by copper.

Soda ash—Sodium bicarbonate (Na_2CO_3). A source of soda in glazes. It is soluble, and hence it is usually used fritted. Also used as an electrolyte.

Sodium chloride—(NaCl). Common salt.

Spodumene—($Li_2O \cdot Al_2O_3 \cdot 4SiO_2$). A flux used in high-fired glazes.

Talc—($3MgO \cdot 4SiO_2 \cdot H_2O$). Pulverized steatite, a flux used in glazes. Its most important use is as a flux in low-fired bodies.

Tin oxide—(SnO_2). The most effective opacifier. Ten percent added to a clear colorless glaze will make it opaque white.

Titanium dioxide—(TiO_2). *See* Rutile.

Umber—A natural source of red iron oxide (Fe_2O_3). Used as a colorant in clay bodies to produce shades of brown.

Uranium—Formerly used as a source of color in glazes. Produces shades of yellow, orange, and red. Used as uranium oxide (U_2O_3).

Vanadium—(V). Used to produce vanadium stain, a yellow colorant for glazes.

Vermiculite—Bloated mica. Used as an insulator in kiln construction.

Volcanic ash—*See* Pumicite.

Wallastonite—A material resembling feldspar with a lower melting point. Used to lower the maturing temperature of clay bodies. Promotes resistance to thermal shock and to crazing.

Water glass—Sodium silicate.

Wax emulsion—A liquid wax used in making wax-resist designs.

White lead—Lead carbonate ($2PbCo_3 \cdot Pb(OH)_2$). The usual source of lead in glazes. POISONOUS.

Whiting—Calcium carbonate ($CaCO_3$). The usual source of calcium in glazes. Used also as a flux in clay bodies.

Yellow base—Vanadium stain.

Zinc oxide—(ZnO). Used as a glaze flux in middle- and high-temperature ranges (above cone 1). When added to low-fired glazes, it produces a mat surface. It is the distinguishing ingredient of Bristol glazes. It affects the colors of other oxides: makes iron dull, makes copper turquoise green, and promotes crystallization in glazes. Zinc oxide should be calcined before use, otherwise it tends to make glazes crawl.

Zirconium—An opacifier similar to tin but not as strong. Twenty percent added to a clear colorless glaze makes it opaque white. Zirconium oxide (ZrO) is too refractory for most glaze use; Zircopax or Opax, commercial silicates of zirconium, are used instead.

Zircopax—*See* Zirconium.

BIBLIOGRAPHY

Ball, F. Carlton and Lovoos, Janice. *Making Pottery Without a Wheel.* New York: Van Nostrand Reinhold, 1965. A comprehensive coverage of hand building. Beautifully illustrated.

Kenny, John B. *Ceramic Design.* Radnor, Pa.: Chilton, 1963. A what-to-do book as well as a how-to-do book. Lots of illustrations.

Leach, Bernard. *A Potter's Book.* London: Faber & Faber; New York: Transatlantic Arts, 1940. An inspirational book. A combination of English and Japanese ideas on pottery.

Lewenstein, Eileen and Cooper, Emmanuel. *New Ceramics.* New York: Van Nostrand Reinhold, 1974. A comprehensive survey of contemporary trends in pottery worldwide. Beautifully illustrated.

Merrill, Virginia and Jessop, Jean. *Needlework in Miniature.* New York: Crown, 1978. Illustrated with 233 photographs, 19 color plates, 64 charts and diagrams.

Newman, Thelma and Merrill, Virginia. *The Complete Book of Making Miniatures for Room Settings and Dollhouses.* New York: Crown, 1975. Illustrated with 700 photographs and 23 color plates.

Newson, Glen C. *Ceramics, A Potter's Handbook.* New York: Holt, Rinehart and Winston, 1971. Comprehensive coverage of ceramics of the past and the present. Section on technical ceramic production.

Rhodes, Daniel. *Clay and Glazes for the Potter.* rev. ed. Radnor, Pa.: Chilton, 1975. A most thorough coverage of the subject.

Index